TORCHBEARER
CHRONICLES

Copyright © 2024 SHINE Books

All rights reserved. No part of this publication may be reproduced, distributed, or transmitted in any form or by any means, including photocopying, recording, or other electronic or mechanical methods, without the prior written permission of the publisher. For permission requests, write to the publisher at the address below.

Some names and identifying details have been changed to protect the privacy of individuals.

Although the authors and publisher have made every effort to ensure that the information in this book was correct at press time, the author and publisher do not assume and hereby disclaim any liability to any party for any loss, damage, or disruption caused by errors or omissions, whether such errors or omissions result from negligence, accident, or any other cause. Furthermore, this book is not intended as a substitute for the medical advice of physicians. The reader should regularly consult a physician in matters relating to his/her health and particularly with respect to any symptoms that may require diagnosis or medical attention.

Book design by Cortney Martinelli.

Editing by Heather Ninni.

Printed in the United States of America.

First printing; 2024.

SHINE Akron LLC

5190 Cline Rd

Kent, Oh 44240

www.shineohio.com

torchbearer

a person who leads or inspires others in working toward a valued state of being

dedicated to

the visionaries, trailblazers and joy-seekers among us.
May you continue to light the way!

There is a light that only you can shine. Your light is unique and vital to the illumination of humanity. Together our lights will brighten the path for others. We do together what we could never do alone.

Shine

Contents

Cortney: Intro … xi

Torchbearer Chronicles

Emily: The Sweet Truth about Being a Business Owner … 1
Mary: Living a Life of Duality … 15
Ted: Love, Create, Play … 33
Danielle: The Awakening … 47
Wesley: The Man Behind the Adventure … 67
Maryanne: Test My Limits or Play it Safe? … 83
Kalyanna: Plot Twist … 103
Beth + Pamela: Yin and Yang … 123
Laura: Imposter Syndrome … 145
Erica: Bouncing Back from Grief and Loss … 165

Follow the Breadcrumbs … 181

Introduction

It was 1982, I was six years old in first grade at a small Christian school in Akron, Ohio. I was born into this school/church. And when I say born into the church, what I mean is that my grandma, who I loved more than anyone in the world, was the church/school secretary. Her and my grandfather were married in the church. My mother was baptized there; my mother and father were married in the church. I was baptized there; my husband and I were married in the church. And my only son was baptized in the church. The church was established in 1877 and had strict, traditional Lutheran roots.

This morning, the principal of the school pulled my small class of a dozen or less into a room, closed the door and excitedly told us that we had an opportunity to make a big difference that day. Our regular teacher was out sick, and we were assigned a substitute teacher. The substitute would be arriving any minute, and it was our mission to make sure she understood how she could be saved and go to heaven. She read from Romans 10:9-10. *"If you confess with your mouth Jesus as Lord and believe in your heart that God raised Him from the dead, you will be saved, for with the heart a person believes, resulting in righteousness, and with the moth he confesses, resulting in salvation."* She went on to give us instruction on what to say and, if we failed in this mission, our substitute teacher would go to hell when she died.

This was the type of language and scenario I became very familiar with over the course of the next two decades as I grew up and became an adult. I want to be clear here, I am not criticizing this church, my principal, or organized religion.

Instead, I am sharing how, as a young child, well-meaning adults told me how I should think, what I should say, and how I should act based on their beliefs. I was not invited to explore my own thoughts or my own beliefs. When I became a mother, at the age of thirty, it was a transformational time in my life, and I was trying to figure out what I believed. As I did this, I tried my best to raise a son who had the space to also think for himself.

This book is about trailblazers, visionaries, healers, and joy-seekers. And I promise you, you don't get to be a trailblazer by thinking like everyone else.

In the pages of this book, you are going to hear from people who are challenging the status quo. People who, through life experiences, have decided to forge their own path. Hopefully they will encourage you to examine some of your ideas and thoughts about life – may their gumption inspire gumption in you.

This book is structured very deliberately. Each chapter contains the story of one author, either in their own words or written by me as the interviewer. In these chapters, you get to take a deep dive into their hearts and minds. What the authors share in this book is their vision, their hopes, their dreams - in less than four-thousand words, packaged in a singular chapter, for all the world to read.

Each story/chapter is followed by a bio and a way to connect with the author, if you so desire.

It is with great honor that I get to provide commentary after each chapter. I do this to shed additional light on their story and their circumstances, from an outside perspective. Additionally, I weave each story together to create one larger story. One of connection. One of love.

It's important to note that although everyone in this book is connected (in ways I probably don't know or even understand), they wrote their chapters as individuals. Each author has their own set of beliefs that may or may not be the same as the other authors in the book. In a symphony, there are harmonic truths that come together in the collective creation, yet the violinist does not have to agree with the flutist to make beautiful music together. The same is true with this book.

I couldn't be prouder of these individuals for their vision, their courage, and their tenacity. If this book was never published; if not one soul ever read a word contained here – the eternal purpose has already been served. As visionaries, trailblazers, and healers, we recognize that the journey is never complete. Our personal growth continues to unfold. We understand that when we reach one apex, there is another in the distance waiting to be realized. The torch we carry is for us alone, and symbolizes our passion for life and that which we yearn to accomplish.

Elizabeth Gilbert, author of the book *Eat Pray Love* – a travel memoir about her spiritual journey that served and inspired millions of people – is quoted as saying, *"Whenever anybody tells me they want to write a book in order to help other people, I always think, Oh, please don't. Please don't try to help me. I mean, it is very kind of you to want to help people, but please don't make it your sole creative motive, because we will feel the weight of your heavy intention. If I sat down to write Eat Pray Love with the sole aim of helping others, I would've produced an entirely different book."*

This book is about *"helping"* **ourselves.**

Not you.

With deepest love,

Cortney

EMILY HARPEL
The Sweet Truth about Being a Business Owner

Emily

The Sweet Truth about Being a Business Owner

I met Emily Harpel in 2023 and instantly became her fangirl. I stalked her (just a little) on social media where she has over 100,000 Instagram followers and 1.3M TikTok followers. I consumed every episode of her podcast *Let Them Eat*, and I read every book she referenced. I thought, "This girl knows something I don't!" and I asked her to be a speaker at our yearly Symposium. But that only whet my appetite. I knew I needed to learn more and was grateful she agreed to be interviewed for this book. After our interview, I realized why I was so smitten with her.

She's real. She's genuine. She's sweet (see what I did there) and kind. She possesses a natural ability and innate confidence that allowed her to build a thriving business right out of college with no 'real' job experience.

So, who is Emily Harpel? She is the founder of Art of Sucre, a Northeast Ohio based luxury cotton candy company. Emily says, "This is not the blue and pink cotton candy that you remember from the fair as a child; instead, it's unique flavors like watermelon, champagne, and peach bellini. You name it, and we've turned it into a cotton candy flavor." Emily is constantly innovating the childhood treat and, as we will learn, it's her thirst for innovation that continues to make her brand relevant.

In 2016, Emily had a single thought (or more appropriately stated – a gut feeling) after her wedding. This feeling led her to what she says is "one of the hardest things she's ever done."

Emily launched Art of Sucre as an events-based business, spinning out-of-the-box flavors of cotton candy at weddings, parties, and concerts. In 2020, Emily had to pivot – BIG TIME – during covid (apparently cotton candy is NOT essential) or lose everything that she worked so hard to build. Fast forward to today, and Emily has completely re-imagined Art of Sucre into an e-commerce powerhouse with her viral cotton candy glitter bombs at the center of the business.

The reimagination didn't come easy during covid. Although Emily admits she felt a sense of relief. Like many people, she had been working non-stop for four years prior to covid. During the "forced long-term vacation," Emily was faced with this internal dialogue: "I built this really cool business that's no longer thriving due to circumstances that are completely out of my control. Can I just let go of this company completely? Do I go and get a real job?" Then, a light bulb went off and Emily realized, "I can't let this idea go!" The scary part was Emily knew she would have to figure out how to take the skill set that she had and move it into something that she knew NOTHING about: e-commerce – packaging, shipping, and logistics. It was a lot more involved than an event-based business. It took her an entire year to get the new business off the ground.

Emily remembers, in the beginning, it was only her. There was nobody else helping drive the business. She worked a lot of back-to-back 20-hour days for nearly a year!

Emily says, "It's so interesting to look back on it now with a little bit of hindsight and some clarity. It almost didn't feel like a choice. I knew I had to do it; it was that simple. I was exhausted. I knew working that many hours was crazy but, at the same time, it didn't feel like I had any other options. It was just what I had to do. Working 20 hours a day didn't feel like a sacrifice to me because I knew what I was working towards, and I knew that it was going to pay off. In fact, I never felt sorry for myself, just the opposite. I felt so lucky that I got to be doing this. During covid, so many of my friends who owned small businesses were not in a place that they were able to pivot. I was able to take this concept that I had worked so hard for and make it even bigger and better. What a gift! I was not going to waste that by feeling sorry for myself when so many other people would have quite literally done anything to be in my shoes."

Emily learned some hard lessons in that first year as she transformed her cotton candy skills into building an e-commerce empire. Looking back, she is truly grateful for those hard lessons, like losing $40,000 on custom branded boxes that didn't secure properly. (Boy, was that a disaster.) Emily says, "As a business owner, nobody can teach you or prepare you for those hard lessons. At the end of the day, you must learn them on your own so that you can come out on the other side as a wiser decision maker."

She knew that she would eventually have to hire experts to do the design work for the packaging and the website because those were outside of her capabilities, and she didn't have time to learn. In the early years, there were ten people spinning and packaging the cotton candy and, Emily admits, they were doing it very inefficiently. Today, with more orders and partnerships, Emily only has three people doing the same work as before.

Emily says one key to her success is spending time doing what comes naturally to her and leaving the rest to someone else. "I still wear a lot of the hats." says Emily. "Now I have people who wear them better than I do." Emily relies on her team to help her execute her business dreams and visions.

Having a team frees Emily up to take on the responsibilities of the business where she naturally thrives. For her, that is creating social media content for TikTok and Instagram. In fact, Emily dedicates up to two and a half days a week to creating content for social media, with the goal of having at least one new video going live every single day.

Half of the work week sounds like a lot of time to dedicate to creating videos, but Emily knows that their social presence drives the brand. Emily says, "We don't pay for any ads whatsoever, all our growth and sales have been 100% organic. You'll hear a lot of businesses talk about their Customer Acquisition Cost, or CAC, and ours is quite literally zero, because we don't pay for it; we don't pay to acquire customers. Especially since I'm the employee who makes the social media content. There's a direct correlation between our sales and how many videos I'm posting daily/weekly."

Social media marketing comes naturally to Emily and it's also what she is most passionate about. It is the part of her job that she loves the most. Emily says, "It is definitely one of my most, if not my most important responsibility as the CEO of my company."

Because she is a trailblazer on the topic, I asked Emily to share the biggest secret we should all know about curating social media content for our businesses. She said, "People look at my brand and see that we have 1.3M TikTok followers and over 100,000 on Instagram. The reality is that the follower count really doesn't matter. What matters is posting consistently, especially with the algorithms. Maybe only 100 people are seeing your videos, but you have no idea who those 100 people might be. One of the viewers could be the CEO of Google. This idea of 'I only have 100 followers' can stop someone from posting. Instead, I tell people to flip their mindset and think, 'Wow, I have one hundred people watching my videos.' When was the last time you had an audience of 100 people? Now you start to realize the impact you can have."

Emily makes it look very easy, but she admits, "Owning a business is very much like being on a roller coaster, the highs are really high, and the lows can be really low and really messy. There have been plenty of times when I have sat on the floor of my office in a full breakdown, crying, not in a good place whatsoever. And then, the next day, I receive an email and I'm on top of the world again. But that's where you see the growth. If things are consistently going well for you - exactly the way that you pictured it - how will you grow? That's just not how life works. It's not realistic at all. And so, what I've tried to do is be as prepared as possible for 'the messy' and then look back at it fondly, knowing it was the catalyst to my growth."

When I asked Emily how she prepares for the messy, she admitted that is something she is naturally wired for. "I'm a problem solver at heart; it's just who I am. If there's an issue, I'm eager to be the one who solves the problem. I'll either execute on the solution myself, or find someone more adept to execute that solution for me."

I asked Emily what it means to be a problem solver. "One of the things that I am coming to realize about myself is that there is this innate sense of confidence within me. I don't question myself when I decide something. Although I may look back at times and feel I didn't make the best decision, I still require myself to follow my gut. The thing is, I don't always need to have all the information to know whether it's a good idea or not. One attribute of a thriving business owner is the ability to make decisions quickly without having all the information." When she witnesses other businesses surveying people off the street for opinions and insights, Emily thinks to herself, "That's not the way to do this. As a business owner you must find your own competence and trust that you can do anything."

So, what does a typical day, partnering with well-known brands such as Kendell Jenner, Barbie, and American Girl look like? Emily says, "The number one thing that I tell people about me is that I'm really boring. I prefer to be at home on my couch with my dog and a book. I think people automatically assume that because I have over a million followers on the internet, I must live a glamorous life. That couldn't be further from the truth. Ninety eight percent of my life is boring. Two percent of my life might be considered glamorous when I'm traveling to New York or LA and bringing my sweet cotton candy treats to people like Beyonce. Most days, I'm staring at a computer."

Emily acknowledges a major factor in the growth of her business (aside from her social media prowess). "Staying innovative is vital to my business," she says. "It is so vital to be consistently innovating and not copying what you see others doing." But how does she manage to consistently innovate? Emily says, "A lot of my creativity comes to me at random times of the day. When that mood strikes, I take advantage of it because I have learned the hard way that I cannot force my creativity. When it comes to me, I will drop EVERYTHING that I'm doing in that moment and focus on the inspiration flowing to me." Emily credits the random streaks of insight for constantly moving her brand and business forward. She's realized that these "big ideas" cannot be forced and that she must remain open and listen when it is sparked. She does that mainly with her yoga practice. This is what keeps her mindful and centered. (I knew I loved this girl!)

Emily admits that this is not something that she can teach to others. "I credit so much of what we've been able to accomplish at Art of Sucre to things that I can't point out or write down on paper as fact. As I mentioned earlier, I credit most of my success to following feelings and gut instincts. It's how I hire my entire team. My interview process is embarrassing. I genuinely don't have a set of questions that I ask people. My partnerships are based off of vibes. I have learned repeatedly that I must trust my gut and it's my superpower as a business owner."

Getting back to the topic of innovation and more importantly 'copying' other people – I asked Emily to talk to me about being inspired by others versus copying others.

"I'm inspired by people all day, every day. I think that's part of what feeds my creativity. I love Pinterest, it's the ultimate platform to be inspired. I fully believe that you should consume content and interact with other people to be inspired. Inspiration and a direct copycat are completely different things and I have experienced both as people have been inspired by me and people have quite literally copied me. I've also done both. I've tried to emulate other creators too. I've tried to emulate this exact version of what somebody else was doing and then realized it never ends well. It doesn't perform well; it doesn't feel right. As opposed to when it's from pure inspiration. If you are directly copying someone you are always going to fall behind. And more importantly, when you copy someone, you are doing yourself a HUGE disservice because you have it in you to be creative and create something that's genuine to you. You must practice flexing those creative muscles to become stronger. It took me until my mid-twenties to really realize that I am 'creative' even though I can't pick up a pencil and draw something beautiful. Creativity comes in a lot of different ways. And this business has allowed me to really flex those muscles and satisfy my creative appetite."

After talking to Emily and hearing her story, two words kept coming to my mind: relentlessness and resiliency. If you aren't willing to become friends with these two words, you might not have what it takes to be a business owner. This is what you need to work endless hours and overcome $40,000 hits to your budget. Emily shared with me that every morning she thinks to herself, "I can't wait to wake up today and do what I do." Like, what is that? I really think it's the human connection that brings Emily joy in such a simple way. Overall, she exudes passion not just for her business but for life. Emily professed to me, "I love talking business. I love owning a business. I love talking to other business owners. I love helping people and giving advice about what I've learned. I love bouncing ideas off other people and watching those ideas become more. These are my favorite things and what really lights a fire in me."

Emily also admits there are things that keep her awake at night. "The wheels in my head are always turning, she says. "The reality is that I don't ever turn that off. I think about how we can continue to be better. How do I continue to grow this brand? How do I continue to keep innovating and being creative? What if I run out of ideas? How do I reach my goals not only for myself, but for my team and for my family? How do I make all this time and energy and sacrifice and commitment worth it in the end? This all sounds like really big, scary stuff. Sometimes it is really big and scary stuff that keeps me up at night. But sometimes it's a sense of pride that I think about when my head hits the pillow. The fact is - I really am proud of myself. Particularly that I was able to pivot the brand. I look at where we have come and hopefully where we are going and try to remember to pat myself on the back sometimes. I know that might sound silly, but I tend to reach a goal and I don't stop to celebrate. Instead, I move right on to the next goal. I've realized I must stop and take time to soak up that success or that win. I really am trying to get better at marinating in the 'win' in real time."

As Emily mentions, some of the late-night ruminating as a business owner is about big and scary things but those thoughts are also the 'life-giving' moments. As a creator myself, that is what I live for; the chance to work through all the thoughts and the ideas. It wouldn't be fulfilling if I had an idea and then executed it perfectly. It's the grit and the messiness that make it life-giving. All business owners can, on some level, agree with this sentiment. For me, it's an honor being kept up at night by these thoughts of how I can make things better and how I can serve.

When the rollercoaster ride takes her on a low, Emily remembers, "I really do believe in myself and if it can happen for somebody else, why can't it happen for me?"

Emily

Emily Harpel is the founder and CEO of Art of Sucre (AOS), a luxury cotton candy company located in Fairlawn, Ohio. In 2016, while on her way home from her honeymoon, Emily decided she was going to give a nostalgic childhood treat a chic upgrade. She secured the social media handles and ordered her first machine, and Art of Sucre was born. AOS began as an events-based business spinning out-of-the-box flavors of cotton candy for weddings, parties, concerts (Hi Arianna and Elton!), and so much more!

In 2020, Emily knew that she either had to pivot her business or lose everything that she worked so hard to build. A year later, Emily re-imagined AOS into an e-commerce powerhouse that now offers nine different unique cotton candy flavors.

What AOS is best known for is their 1.3M TikTok followers of their viral Cotton Candy Glitter Bombs. Emily has also built her business by partnering with national brands such as Barbie, American Girl, Kate Spade, 818, and more!

How to connect with Emily
Tik Tok and Instagram: artofsucre
Website: https://artofsucre.com/

MARY LOVE
Living a Life of Duality

Mary

Living a Life of Duality

To be a torchbearer is to lead by holding the light through an ignited form of love in your soul, illuminating the way of others. In my world, I hold a burning flame with a long stick of adversity triumphed as a resilient woman in my thirties. I raise my light high for onlookers to spot me, miles and miles away. Selflessly, I embody heightened energy and harness integrity in everything I do. It intrigues many when I tell them I am a molecular biologist, author, blogger, yogi, meditation teacher, psychic medium, and overall spiritual person. In introducing my memoir, *Borrowed Wings*, I touch on my adult life as a scientist and spiritual being. Life for me, with this lens, has been an energetically rewarding human experience.

Since I was a little girl, I have had experiences with the spiritual world that I translate through clairvoyant experiences. Coined in the late seventeenth century, clairvoyance is defined as clear seeing through extrasensory perceptions and/or images outside of the natural eye vision. Two main types of clairvoyance exist, internal and external. Internal clairvoyance is seen through your third eye, or your mind's eye. I experience internal clairvoyance when I am speaking with someone, and images containing additional information about the person appear in my mind's eye. Since the age of five, I saw spirits such as my stepfather in full form, as if they were standing behind a cloud of smoky energy. The first time I saw my stepfather from an externally clairvoyant perception was the night after finding out he was no longer alive. He stood in the doorway of my bedroom as we exchanged looks, yet I was unafraid of his spirit form. I am grateful for these experiences and my ability to tap into this sixth sense. I have learned to carry this intuition forward in everything I do, including my work as a scientist.

My educational background is in molecular biology and chemistry, but my industry experience is mostly in immunology. Immunotherapy is a type of treatment where immune cells help the body fight an indication such as cancer, sickle cell, or asthma. What makes immunotherapy more complex, personalized, or different than biological treatments, such as chemotherapy, is the composition and how it targets the indication. Immunotherapy products are made from cells, organs, or tissues that are compatible with the patient. Composition of immunotherapy products could be autologous (your own cells), or allogeneic (e.g., compatible donor cells or universal O Neg donor cells). Immunotherapy is considered a new science, and I love being on the leading edge of discoveries.

For my undergraduate research, I studied tyrosine kinase proteins and signaling within the body that are intricate in cellular communication at a molecular level. For my graduate research, I focused on viruses and different methods for cells to be re-engineered into cancer killing machines.

I am currently the head of Manufacturing Sciences & Technology for a biotech company in New Jersey, focused on early phase immunotherapy trials. As a scientist, I not only oversee the scientists, engineers, and laboratories that translate experimental designs into clinical trial ready protocols, but I am the gatekeeper between the development and manufacturing space. I wear many hats at work. Whether I am on a business call, training staff members in the laboratory, or consulting with companies on cell therapy products – each day is exciting as I get to be part of decisions that impact lives on the other side of immunotherapy products.

My openness about my "double life" which I purposely use double quotes, as I only live one life – did not happen until my mid-twenties. Until then, I did not speak publicly about my psychic and mediumship abilities. It was right after my prefrontal cortex development at the age of twenty-five that I began to share the dichotomy of my life with others. Not only is there a duality to my life, but there is a duality to my writing, as you may find in this chapter. Understanding the world of energy has fed a balanced brain, mind, spirit, and soul experience that makes the world magnificent. Being a medium, a term I did not know existed until adulthood, took years for me to understand as I healed from a traumatic childhood.

The trauma I experienced in childhood started at birth. I was conceived through infidelity when my married parents (to other people) had me after years of being friends "with benefits". My stepfather and mother separated when I was five, and soon after, my stepfather committed suicide. My mother fell into a deep depression and substance abuse for several years, which led to a slew of issues with abuse, neglect, and hatred towards my existence. I raised myself with the help of my community, friends, their parents, following my intuition and listening to spirit guides. Child protective services came to my house several times throughout my upbringing, after reports of me not eating for days at a time, sexual abuse, physical abuse markings, and others. In my early teenage years,

I began developing addictions to drinking, sex, and drugs. My mother and I fought constantly, and eventually I was removed from my home and placed in foster care at age fifteen. My healing journey started in foster care when I discovered yoga and meditation at the Brahma House shelter. Through moving around and losing two years' worth of school credits, I figured out how to graduate on time. Afterward, I went to college and focused on my education and building my adult life. From that day, I vowed to continue to cater to my spirit, in continual maintenance of my health, healing, and asking for professional help when I need it.

Because of my volatile upbringing, it was important for me to sense security in my career and the world around me before making my duality public knowledge. Not to mention, I did not fully understand spirituality myself, so I lacked the words to articulate it to others.

When I announced my ability to connect to spirits on social media and to friends, it was so freeing for all the parts of me to finally come together. I could navigate the world without hiding who I truly was. Until college, only my closest friends knew about my clairvoyance and foresight.

It was my husband, Peter, who made me feel normal, just as I am.

In the summer, going into my sophomore year of college, I started dating Peter. This was a coming-of-age time for me, as it was also the first summer of me not living within the foster care system. Life in foster care was a fresh wound. It had only been a year since I had moved out of the Passages independent living program, which was an extension of Brahma House.

That first summer of freedom led to spontaneously planned trips. Living in northern New Jersey for college was exciting because there was so much to see in upstate New York and New Jersey that I had never seen before. One day, after a long trip to the beach, I stayed over at Peter's house for the first time. In the morning, I found myself in front of Peter's dresser looking at a vintage relic motorcycle statue. A thought crossed my mind to pick it up and, in my head, I instantly heard a voice that wasn't mine say, *"Do not touch that, it's mine,"* as a smoky gray, semi translucent spirit appeared to the left of me.

I had not seen a spirit this vividly since high school. With widened eyes and an anxious jump, the spirit disappeared. Peter took note of my surprise and reaction to the spirit.

In his stern Brooklyn accent, he said, "Are you okay?" Facing the mirror, I stared at him without turning around. I must have appeared like a deer in headlights.

"Yes. Hi, good morning." I said.

"What did you see just now?" We locked our eyes in the mirror and shared a few seconds of silence. Peter likely knew. I cleared my throat.

"I thought I saw something in the corner of my eye, but it was nothing." Hoping to change the subject, I responded with a gentle smile. I walked to bed and crawled back in. He embraced me, and I took a deep breath.

"I know what you saw, but why don't you just tell me?" To keep a poker face, I smiled, then quickly frowned. My solar plexus felt hollow, which is my intuitive signal that the conversation about my ability to see spirits was about to surface.

I said, "I was looking at your dresser and I saw a spirit next to me, and he said not to touch the motorcycle statue because it was his." I took another deep breath in terror at the potential reaction. My immediate assumption was that Peter would judge me.

He said, "That is my uncle. But how did you see him? What did he look like to you?"

"He appeared smoky but about my height, looked Spanish, and thin."

"Wow, you saw him clear like that? Let me show you what he looks like. On the other side of the room, he grabbed a photo frame of his uncle and his mother. When Peter handed it to me, I nodded with widened eyes.

"That's him. Exactly like that."

"Wow. I did not think anyone could see him the way I can. You can see clearly. That's pretty good." I giggle in thought of this time because *pretty good* meant a serious compliment. When I recently told Peter about how my spirit guide advised a client on how to help a person wake up from a year-long coma and the timing in which it would happen, he said those same words when it all came to fruition in that exact manner.

Pretty good Mary, good job.

From that moment, Peter and I have been able to communicate with each other about our experiences in the spiritual realm. It enhances our relationship and allows us to build an authentic life together. Many are unaware of Peter's spiritual gifts, so it feels like a special secret that we share together. I am thankful to have him as a supportive person in my life, and a partner that understands the spiritual world like I do.

During college in the late 2000s, my roommates knew about my intuition at surface level, but I never explained my encounters as a child.

After college and entering the adult workforce, I started to explore what it felt like to have conversations with others about spirits. It took a few years, but I finally began to announce to others at work that I was a psychic medium. Many of my colleagues who were unfamiliar with mediumship seemed intrigued and began asking me all sorts of questions to understand more.

For those who already knew of my dual life and interests, they were pleased that I began sharing this second aspect of my life with others. When I "came out" on social media, one friend texted me, *'finally'*. After sharing this announcement with the world, there was an adjustment period for me as I figured out how to live in this new way. People began seeing me through a new lens and it took time to acclimate to those new relationships and conversations. But it gave me an opportunity to heal parts of myself and fully embody who I am. From that moment forward, I stood firm, fully embracing the real me.

I am still questioned by my scientific colleagues about giving psychic readings, my thoughts on spirits, or connecting to individuals in comas or who have transitioned through death. Often people are surprised at how "normal" I am given my childhood and these psychic abilities. I credit this to yoga and meditation, where I have learned how to tap into my inner self and heal related trauma.

On an atomic, elemental, molecular, and ionic level, the basics of chemistry support the notion that everything we endure in the human experience is also metaphysical. Let's start by recognizing the Law of Conservation of Mass, which states that energy cannot be created or destroyed. Energy is everywhere and its laws are not only chemistry, but quantum mechanics, biochemistry, and physics. If we look at basic principles, elements create compounds and compounds have physical properties that depend on the reaction of chemical changes. Compounds, which are molecules that build the human body and earth around us, react to changes in the environment. If I carry a negative mindset throughout the day, there is a higher chance to energetically bleed the negativity to the people and spaces around me. Let's take the food I consume as an example. The digestion of the food will either yield molecules that are beneficial or detrimental to my body depending on my mindset about that food.

Let's look at basic chemistry, where atoms interact with neighboring electron clouds, orbital portals, from other atoms or molecules. Everything initially interacts through the atom's electron cloud, leading to changes in state (ground versus excited), larger conglomerates, and the creation of a stable molecule like water or salt. Every molecular atom, element, human, and being in between that, wants stability. By this basic desire of wanting to be stable, vibration and energy come into play. Trillions of atoms interact with one another to keep the elements, molecules, systems, and hence, our human bodies stable. It is so simple but so complex.

When we think of the kinetic molecular theory, the law that the average kinetic energy (KE) of anything as gas form is proportional to the absolute temperature of gas in Kelvin. To break this down into layman's terms, KE = (mass) x (speed) 2 x (0.5), where speed moves quick compared to molecular masses (e.g., gas particles). For instance, walking into a busy room with people you've never met, and the entire room stops and stares at you. Your KE, in this case, wouldn't be your human body, but spiritually, it is the energy you carry in your outer sheaths/aura. I share this scenario with you because I believe KE is part of how we harness clairvoyance, clairaudience, and claircognizance.

I have a theory that extends to how remote viewing works, as well. Remote viewing is the ability to clairvoyantly assess people, objects, places, and scenarios in distant locations. It is known that the Central Intelligence

Agency experimented with remote viewing during wars in the 20th century, where they would attempt to receive information from the enemy for their advantage. I believe the KE works through the outer sheaths to allow remote viewing, which allows human beings to see ahead and backward in time.

The basics and foundations of general scientific principles are critical in finding the answer, but also a tool in reworking someone's mindset. Scientists have yet to publicly document, prove, or explain how we can connect to spirit. Through extensive research, scientists have discovered that at the surface level of spirituality how meditation and yoga can lead to feelings of peace, improved health, and a positive outlook on life. However, no one has published a peer-reviewed article or scientific journal that breaks down the methods of spiritually connecting to spirits or unraveling clairvoyance.

I remember in both undergraduate and graduate school; professors pausing their trail of thought in class because they could not fully explain something. Rather, they would say it was an act of God. Concepts like the synchrony of molecules working together in trillions to ensure one's hand can physically grab a cup is just one example.

Molecules are at work within us, and the brain runs the show between the physical and spiritual realms. Scientifically speaking, the suprachiasmatic nucleus manages the circadian rhythm and is located in the brain. The circadian rhythm is our cell's biological clock, that operates in sync. Complexity lives in the trillions of cells moving in synchrony to create every movement we make, thought we have, and translations to speak. I believe feelings of intuition, or subconscious thoughts, are also synchronized with our mind, similar to the physical cells. Divine energy acts somewhere here.

It's taken some time, but I now love and embrace the duality of my life. I've realized that one aspect doesn't make the other less true or real. I am a woman who is both spiritual and scientific; technical and open-minded. My gifts have shaped me into the woman I am today. The duality of science and spirituality reminds me of the bodies of water that surround the land formation on earth. Researchers have studied the ocean floors and identified the species that live within, but there is so much unknown that lingers throughout the ocean. Many people love the ocean because it makes us feel tranquil. I love to reflect as the water washes up on the beach. We may never know everything there is to know about the ocean, but so many are drawn to live and visit there. I feel the same way about energy and vibration. I may not know how it works scientifically, but I still have a desire to visit and access the world of spirituality.

Mary

Mary Love is a molecular biologist, an advocate for abuse survivors, keynote speaker, writer, and spiritual frontrunner. She founded Spiritual Atlas, a wellness and advocacy-based limited liability company in New Jersey.

Through Spiritual Atlas, she offers meditation workshops, yoga classes, readings, and promotes spiritual wellness through bridging scientific principles of energy and vibration. Mary is the author of two books, a memoir, and a poetry essay collection on the Human Experience. She is an avid field hockey player, skier, and yogi.

When she's not adulting or writing, she works closely with the State of New Jersey's Department of Children and Families and associated organizations to help youth, spread awareness on building resilience and policy. She and her husband Peter have two cats and live in New Jersey.

How to connect with Mary:
Website: https://www.spiritualatlas.com
Instagram: spiritual_atlas11
Twitter: spiritual_atlas
Facebook: spiritualatlas

Narration on Mary
with Cortney

You have the gift to translate potential

Are you aware of your five senses? Are you aware of why they exist, aside from allowing you to smell, taste, touch, hear, and see?

They exist to translate energy.

Your five senses are translating mechanisms. It is with these senses that you translate the world of vibration and frequency all around you. You are so good at translating vibration; you don't even know you are doing it. You see the color green because your eyes are translating light waves that are vibrating at 555 THz per second. You hear a hummingbird because your ears are translating the sound wave that is vibrating at 80 Hz per second.

Your five senses essentially translate what has been manifested. But you could also just as easily translate that which has yet to manifest. That which is potential. That which is within the field of consciousness. Sometimes referred to as the Akasha.

According to scientists, our five sense only translate fifteen percent of the vibration and frequencies all around us. Everything is vibration and energy. Everything is oscillating in motion and can be measured.

For example, we know our microwaves are omitting a frequency even though we don't see, taste, smell, hear, or touch it. The same is true for our cell phones and x-ray machines.

As young children, we often used our sixth sense – until well-meaning adults talked us out of it. Those well-meaning adults only wanted us to translate what was concrete, tangible, and manifested. Slowly but surely, we stopped cultivating this awareness all together. It became so quiet, or even silenced – we no longer experienced it.

And now, as adults, many people find me and ask me to help them tap into their intuition, their sixth sense. Often, people think this is something you are either born with or not. But the truth is, we were ALL born with it. We just have to cultivate what we once lost.

These are the five common ways people access their intuition or sixth sense:
- CLAIRVOYANCE: Seeing without the eyes – visions – translating through the third eye
- CLAIRAUDIENCE: Hearing words or sounds not with your ears – thought form that you translate with your own words, through your filters
- CLAIRALIENCE: Smelling – translating energy with our sense of smell
- CLAIRCOGNIZANCE: A Knowing – you know something, but you can't explain why
- CLAIRSENTIENCE: A Feeling – a feeling takes place usually in your solar plexus or another part of your physical body

Most people, after hearing these five common ways, usually resonate with one or more. I bet you have had a "gut feeling," or a strong knowing even though you weren't sure where it was coming from – that is your sixth sense!

And if you want to, you can cultivate it. It's your birthright.

TED SENF
Love, Create, Play

Ted

Love, Create, Play

I sat down with my spiritual teacher, Ted, to ask him a few questions. There was no way I could write a collaborative book on Torchbearers, Healers, and Visionaries and not have Ted in it. Like always, when sitting down with Ted, I never know where the conversation will go. Enjoy as you read the words of a true living master.

Cortney: Let's just jump in with something you said to me recently when we were having one of our daily talks about life. You said to me, "Growth is Messy." You've said a lot of brilliant things to me over the last two decades, but this one I can't shake. Let's talk more about this.

Ted: Yes, if I recall, you had some transitions going on in your life and even though you "asked" for that change, it was requiring some difficult conversations and actions on your part.

Cortney: Yes, that's right.

Ted: Growth implies I'm going from one place to another place. And getting to the other place typically requires letting go of something else so you can make space for something new, right? I have to let go of where I am. And I have to start moving to where I want to be. And that can get messy.

Cortney: You have to crack some eggs to make an omelet.

Ted: Yes, of course – and part of the joy of life is when you start embracing the mess because you recognize it for what it is. It's the clay we get to play with. When you recognize it for its purpose, for the gift that it is (even though it's messy), there's a little bit of anticipation. You start to ask questions like, "Ooh, what's coming out of this? Where am I going with this?" You start to get curious.

Cortney: Yes, I love this shift in mindset, because anyone can do it with practice. You always tell me, "Get fascinated, instead of frustrated." I use this a lot when I notice myself getting frustrated with something or someone. I deliberately shift it to, "Why is this person's perspective fascinating, what can I learn from this person's point of view?" Once I shift, what comes from that is a beautiful interaction.

Ted: Let's apply this concept of 'growth is messy' to relationships. Most of us think the perfect relationship is when everybody gets along all the time. That's not what we want. That's a stagnant relationship. It's the relationships that get messy AND when both people know how to clean up a mess in the right way, that's thriving, that's growing, that is life-giving and that is what makes us a better person in the process. Wish for that relationship - one where mess happens, but both people are in such a good place that growth comes out of the mess.

Cortney: How can both people be in a good place so that growth can come out of it?

Ted: By being selfish and taking care of yourself first and taking the time to feel good. You have a tenet at Shine that speaks to this: "When you feel good, you do good." It's brilliant.

Cortney: Oddly enough, this conversation that we are having reminds me of a quote from my favorite movie, *The Notebook*. I know it's cheesy, but I love the quote, "The best love is the kind that awakens the soul and makes us reach for more, that plants a fire in our hearts and brings peace to our minds." I always heard this quote and thought, yeah, it's the relationships that are passionate and awakening something inside of us that are the good ones. The messy ones.
At the age of 75, you seem to just get younger and younger – more passion, more pep in your step. What continues to drive you towards your mission? What is it that keeps you young and vibrant? What fuels you?

Ted: Feeling good

Cortney: Feeling good?

Ted: Yeah, absolutely. To me, that's at the top of the list every day. Because if I'm not feeling good, I'm off track. And when I'm off track, life is not flowing.

Cortney: Are you saying that everything you do is so that you can feel good? Is that what you're saying?

Ted: Yes, because if I'm not feeling good, again, I'm off track. So why would I be motivated to do anything if it doesn't feel good? I'm going to go through periods of messiness, like we just talked about, because that's part of life. But I don't want to stay there. Actually, I don't HAVE to stay there. And I don't want my whole life to be a mess, right? I want to be able to mess, create, mess, create, mess, create. It's like the artist creating a beautiful painting. There's a mess before the art is complete. As a human, the earlier that I can detect the mess, the quicker I can start creating.

Cortney: Ok, so how can we start to feel good regularly? Help us understand this.

Ted: Absolutely. As you know, the first ritual I do before I even get out of bed, as my conscious thoughts are starting to flow in, is I put my hands over my heart and I say, "Another day, to love, to create, to play – thank you." I will not get out of bed until I *feel* those words. It's not enough to say the words, I have to really feel them. One of my goals each day is to be able to love freely. Even if I don't see another human that day, I still get to love. I can send love anywhere on the planet and beyond.

Cortney: You talked about rituals. And you are the master of rituals. I've never met anyone in my life who has more rituals in place than you. And being so close to you, I know that is probably one of the biggest driving factors to your alignment (besides your imagination, which we will get to shortly). But what if you woke up one day and didn't want to do a ritual? What if it felt like a chore instead of something that made you feel good?

Ted: That's a great question! Often, when I teach people about rituals, they think, "Oh this is just another thing I have to add to my 'to do' list." For me - and this is important - if a ritual is no longer making me happy, then I'd stop doing it because it would no longer be serving me. Everything has a life. What you used to do might not work for you now, as the person you've become or are becoming. It's ok to re-evaluate what you are doing. The only thing permanent is our existence. Everything else has a shelf life, and that's perfectly fine. There's nothing wrong with that.

Cortney: What happens when we don't let go of the things when they are no longer bringing us joy or happiness? What happens when the shelf life expires but we hang on?

Ted: That's kind of the definition of burnout - insisting on doing something after it has ceased feeling good to you.

Cortney: Ok, this is good. This is what I want to ask you. I know your purpose in life is to 'serve others well'. What if that ceased to bring you happiness? What if the shelf-life expired? You would be able to give yourself permission to let that go?

Ted: Yes, I would feel obligated to let it go, and here's why. If it wasn't serving me, it wouldn't be serving them. That's a rather obvious statement, but it's true.

Cortney: Oh, wait, say that again.

Ted: If it wasn't serving me, it wouldn't be serving them.

Cortney: That's big. Can you talk more about that?

Ted: Once you begin doing something and it doesn't feel good to you, it's going to have a different vibration. It's the difference between serving and sacrificing. Being of service is a fluid, liquid, self-replenishing process. Sacrificing is depleting and has a heaviness to it. And even the person you are sacrificing for takes on some of that burden, knowingly or unknowingly. When you sacrifice for others, it might appear that you are doing them good, but it's an illusion. In the long run, it is a burden for both people involved.

Cortney: My mind is blown! I've never heard you say it in this way before. Everything has a frequency, and the frequency between serving and sacrificing is huge!

Ted: Huge.

Cortney: So, you can literally be doing the same act, but, depending on your intention, the Universe feels it differently.

Ted: Yes, same act. But it is a different frequency and therefore the person will feel it in a different way. If Brian came home tonight and gave you flowers and said, "I saw these flowers and I thought of you and just had to get them for you," that is a very different frequency then if it was Valentine's Day and he felt obligated to buy them for you. Same flowers. Different frequency. And every act and its frequency ripples out into the Universe.

Cortney: I want to get back to your morning ritual of you saying and feeling, "Another day, to love, to create, to play – thank you." We've talked about the love and the creating - what does the play look like?

Ted: Play, that's just all about having fun! Laughing. Enjoying life and not taking it so seriously. Not feeling like there must be a point or a purpose to everything. Just doing things for the sake of fun. I have a cat, named Zen...

Cortney: Of course you do...

Ted: Zen loves to play chase. And I just laugh...chasing him around. He'll hide and wait for me to come around the corner. Or I'll throw something he'll go chase it. We have a great time. If I'm watching TV in the evening, I'm going to watch something that's going to make me laugh. I will not let the last thing I watch put me in a serious mood. I just can't do that. Having fun is so innate in who we are. Children live their life that way. Their only thought is where's the fun, right? Animals also get that. They just want to play and have fun. So, yes, play is a big part of my life. Those three things: love, create, and play. What if you built those three things into every relationship you had? That's going to be a pretty darn good relationship.

Cortney: Since we are talking about play, let's talk about your imagination. Your imagination is incredible and it's also how you create.

Ted: One day you turned to me and said, "That's your superpower, imagination." And it just clicked on every level. Every cell of my being said, "Of course! We've been trying to tell you that your entire life." But when you said those words, it was like magic. My imagination is my superpower. It is how I create.

Cortney: Can you please share the Einstein quote about this?

Ted: Einstein said, *"Imagination is more important than knowledge."* Knowledge is limited. Imagination is infinite. Infinite. How can I change anything without imagining it to be different first? We are using our imagination all the time. Usually, it's to create things we don't want. We imagine how things could go wrong. We imagine the worst outcomes and then wonder why it's happening. What if we unleashed our imagination to create the things we want? That is what you unleashed in me. I use it much more deliberately now than I ever have. And it's so fun.

Cortney: This makes me think of another point I would like to make. Our strengths are so inherent in us that we often don't realize that they are there. We think everyone thinks like us, but they don't.

Ted: Yes, another good point. Your strength is probably something you do so naturally that you don't even realize it's a game changer. Once you identify a strength, like you did for me, suddenly you start doing it purposefully and deliberately. Now it really is your superpower! I mean, what's the point of having a superpower if you don't know how to use it?

Cortney: And that's a great gift we can give to the people we love. Reflect to them their superpowers.

Ted: Yes, identify it for them. Catch people doing something that really makes a difference consistently.

Cortney: Since we are on this topic of relationships and speaking faith into other people, let's circle back and talk about your mantra of 'serving others well'. What does that look like for you?

Ted: It's not a mental process for me because if I must plot out and plan and strategize about how to be of service to you, now I'm getting into the area of sacrifice. To get into that state of serving others well, it's a state of flow. And a state of flow is very creative. It means I'm not going to dictate what's going to happen. It's just going to flow and all I have to do is hold that space of love and allow it to play out without interfering. What I realized when you pulled my Human Design chart is that I am fully alive and fully connected when I am in service to others. And you can't be a genuine service to another without the Universe simultaneously being of service to you.

Cortney: Yes, it is no accident that your Incarnation Cross in Human Design is Right Angle Cross of Service.

Ted: I was reading a chapter in a book years ago and the author said, "If you want something, you should start giving it away without any expectation of what's coming back." Folks, it's never about something I'm getting, it's always about something I'm not giving.

Cortney: Please give us a specific example.

Ted: Okay. So, let's say I'm in a work environment, and I don't feel appreciated. If I could just get a moment of clarity around that, my mission would be to catch people doing things right and appreciate them. And I would never have to worry about being appreciated ever again. Give it away. Give appreciation away.

Cortney: Wow, I love that! Whatever it is that you're not getting, you need to deliberately acknowledge it and then decide you're going to give it to other people.

Ted: Give it away. Give it away.
Here's another example. Let's say I'm in a relationship and I don't feel like I'm getting love. And then you start comparing who's doing what. If I am giving you love with the expectation of you loving me back, that is sacrifice. That is a business agreement. Love by its truest, purest nature, is just giving. It has nothing to do with receiving. I can step back at a moment of clarity, and think to myself, "I'm going to love this person because I love them. And I'm not going to have any expectation of what is going to come back." There's a principle in the Universe that every tradition teaches: Karma, Law of Attraction, What Comes Around Goes Around, The Golden Rule.

Cortney: Since this book is about Trailblazers and Visionaries, can you share with us what qualities you think these people have that other people don't?

Ted: Yes, I think there are visionaries out there, and I think you're one of them, who have a little bigger, more defined set of desires than the average person.

Cortney: Interesting, you think it's a defined desire?

Ted: Yeah, there's a desire in them, that when they imagine it, they're not going to stop. They are going to put all of their deliberate attention into making it happen. They're going to be consistent with it, until it just must be. It must manifest in some way or another. Trailblazers and visionaries are relentless. They must be, because it's not easy to go where no one has gone before. It's an unpaved road, so there's going to be a lot that comes up on the path to distract them or discourage them. Like I said, they have a bigger, defined desire.

Cortney: What is the best advice you have ever given and what is the best advice you have ever been given?

Ted: Well, I have to say, advice is overrated. It's much more about acknowledging people than advising people. The best advice they could ever get is already within them. You are just creating a space where they can hear their own advice. Have the patience to allow the mud to settle and the water to clear. You help them settle. You help them get still in that stillness. Then, the clarity moves in, and they have their own answer.

Cortney: Probably the most profound statement I've heard you make. And that's what our relationship has been for the past 15 years. Is there anything else you want to say before we end our time together?

Ted: Just three words: Love. Create. Play.

Ted

For the last 15 years of his career, **Ted Senf** dazzled the corporate world with his words of wisdom as an Education Consultant and Keynote speaker. Now retired, he offers spiritual guidance to like-minded seekers. He shares with the singular goal of "serving others well." Ted is also a popular TEDx Akron speaker.

Ted's latest project of passion is being the co-creator and co-lead of the Vibration Mastery Program™, a six-month program where students are taught and experience a new way of living through the teachings of energy and vibration. This program begins every year in October, where a dozen new spiritual seekers take a journey to a sacred (internal) place as an act of spiritual devotion.

How to connect with Ted
Email: tedsenf@windstream.net
Vibration Mastery Program™:
www.shineakron.com/vibration-mastery-program

DANIELLE HUNTER
The Awakening

"My dear friend, I may be the victim of wrong perceptions, and what I write here may not reflect the truth. However, this is my experience of the situation. This is what I really feel in my heart. If there is anything wrong in what I write, let us sit down and look into it together so that we can clarify the misunderstanding."

– Thich Nhat Hanh

Danielle

The Awakening

Sitting in a fire-engine-red Adirondack chair near the small garden where I had picked a vibrant yellow squash the day before, I faced toward the back of my two-story home with burnt orange bricks, charcoal gray siding, and white metal awnings over the upstairs windows. I gazed upward to the late-afternoon sky and followed the sun's rays to the glistening water of the oversized above-ground pool. The rhythmic buzzing of cicadas was streaming in and out of my ears in what felt like a cleansing of my brain, going in one ear and out the other and back again. It was a cacophony of sounds connecting me to nature, to my source. *The Yoga Sutras of Patanjali* sat in my lap, pages dog-eared and marked up with underlined words, stars, and arrows from a No. 2 pencil to emphasize the insights and revelations during my reading sessions under the warm embrace of Ohio's July sunshine.

The book is an essential read for anyone taking a journey on the spiritual path, and one that I had been studying for several days. What stood out at that moment were the teachings of non-attachment. I had wondered why anyone would want to detach from their identity and their loved ones, particularly their own children. I found joy spending time with my two daughters and watching them grow, my two dogs from the time they were puppies, our home that we had settled into a few years before, my various creative pursuits, and the community of like-minded yogis I had joined the year prior. Yet, I was open to pondering this notion of non-attachment. I closed my eyes, started to follow my breath, and surrendered to the thought of being unattached and truly present.

Breathing in, sensing the blood whooshing in and out from the center of my chest; breathing out, hearing the air flow through my throat like ocean waves in a seashell. Breathing in, filling my body from the oxygen of the trees that surrounded me; breathing out, reciprocating the gift of life. Breathing in the universe; breathing out into infinity.

I didn't know where my body ended as the sensation of my skin dissolved into the air that surrounded me. There was a stillness I hadn't experienced before, the space between the breaths. It was quiet but there was a faint hum. A profound sense of knowing washed over me as I became unattached from my life, yet completely connected and absorbed into the universe. I saw my entire existence from a new perspective and didn't recognize who I had become.

No one knows what's behind the smile of another. Behind my smile was unhappiness with the negativity and pain from a relationship with a man who I had once believed would keep me safe from anything negative or painful. While motherhood was my light, I felt so lonely with few meaningful adult conversations like the ones I had with friends on late nights during my time at college. Yet, I continued to have late nights throughout the years anxiously waiting and wondering where the father of my children was, how much he had to drink, and what time he would come home or turn in for the night. There were countless times I would wake in the dead of night to peer out the window to see if his vehicle was parked safely in our driveway and feel a rush of dread pour out from my stomach when I saw nothing. I can still remember what it felt like in those moments when my heart pumped in my chest, face tingling, as clammy fingers pressed the buttons on my phone to call him. I never knew which version of him would be on the other end of the call; if he answered at all.

Despite many nights alone with the children, the excuses that followed, and an endless list of heartbreaking experiences, I chose to stay because that's what you do – you keep the family together, right? For better, for worse. I took the vow and always believed if I pushed hard enough, yelled enough, cried enough, change would be possible. And when that didn't work, there came a point when I became complacent and strived for contentment in my marriage.

"Give thanks to those great spiritual teachers (parents, spouse, children, neighbors, etc.)... they let you know each day how much more work you truly have to do and in what ways you have not mastered yourself." – Dr. Wayne Dyer

Although I wasn't experiencing the peace I wanted in my life, I permitted myself to be content with my circumstances. In doing so, I dimmed my light. The person I had become was only a quiet shadow of who I really was. *But who was I really?* I saw someone who was broken and voiceless with little freedom to grow while walking on eggshells to avoid as much confrontation as possible. She had to keep herself small and was perpetually drained, fearful, and confused. She suffered from internal battle wounds, and dealt with years of anxiety, panic attacks, and a plethora of health issues with no diagnosable cause. Her thoughts and worries were repeatedly expressed to the one person who she thought could make it all better, but he either didn't listen or didn't care.

It's hard to see this truth as I look back at the collection of happy photos I captured, documenting all of the good moments to share with others. For over 15 years, I put on a smile and obsessively curated the perfect life for everyone on the outside to see, while feeling worthless on the inside and pouring all my angry and sad thoughts into the multiple journals and notebooks I kept.

Jostled by my reality, words rang in my ears... *Why are you staying here? There is so much more to life. Nothing is ever going to change. You've tried your hardest to fix it all. It's time to let go of this life and start over.*

The Decision

This spontaneous moment of non-attachment and complete absorption during meditation awoke a deep truth within my soul. I saw my entire existence through the eyes of an outsider and the thought that I could fix my marriage ceased to exist. My soul finally knew it was time to make a decision. Was I going to continue living an unhappy, unfulfilled life or do I flush it all away and start over? The choice was simple. I chose me, my daughters, and a path toward the peace, love, and happiness that we all deserve.

I secretly planned my exit strategy; packed what I could and only informed a small circle of people close to me. During that treacherous two-week period, I continued the charade of a happy wife like I had done all those previous years. I knew if my secret got out, grave consequences could unfold.

On Thursday, July 27th, 2017, my parents arrived at the home that would no longer be *my* home. An overwhelming sense of sadness, anger, and pity were all wrapped up within me. Nauseousness filled the pit of my stomach and there was a tightness deep within my chest, followed by a squeezing that crept in around my throat. Fear and dread were prevalent, hoping that we wouldn't be caught as we hurriedly packed up my minivan and parents' sedan. I pulled out of the driveway, tears welled up and streamed down my face as I said goodbye to the home, friends, and community I grew to love, ultimately taking my girls across state and away from the life that they had always known.

As I drove farther and farther away from it all, there was something pulling me towards my roots as I watched my old life vanish in the rearview mirror. I knew I had to keep moving forward to experience the growth and peace I was seeking. I had to start a new life. I wanted to live with authenticity. I had to do this for myself. I had to do this for my girls. There was no turning back. My intention was to let go and surrender to what the universe would provide. Although I only had $20 to my name, I felt empowered to show my daughters a strong, independent woman. I would provide them with love, stability, and positivity. I wanted what was best for everyone and had to reconstruct the pieces of a shattered family to create a better life. I never believed I would be starting over from the bedroom of my childhood home.

Rebuilding

If you had asked me several years ago if I would ever work as a human resources professional, I would have laughed in your face. I had grown to seek the safety of my solitude and motherhood and didn't feel worthy of being respected or finding success in a career. Yet, in this next phase of my life, I was full of determination and drive to face my fears in my search to find full-time work. After applying to multiple jobs, a month into my new life, I was finally offered an assistant position in the Human

Resources department at a local non-profit organization.

I felt like I was coming of age and starting from the bottom in an entry-level position, knowing that this wasn't beneath me despite my education and bachelor's degree. I had a sense of curiosity and began to learn about my strengths and weaknesses and worked on them both. Lacking adult networking skills for so many years, I felt awkward, like an imposter, worried about sounding stupid, thinking people were judging me, or that I would vomit out a word salad while going off on tangents. But I kept persisting and had to nurture my communication and customer service skills while being a late-blooming professional.

Each day I showed up, both at work and at home, and while finding solace in my yoga and meditation practice, I progressed faster than I could imagine. My 200-hour Yin Yoga certification had begun and encouraged me to come to an uncomfortable edge and find stillness within not only my body, but in all aspects of my being. I found myself expanding in the meditative and therapeutic practice of Yin Yoga where healthy tissues and balanced qi are the priority, not the aesthetically aligned poses that one may imagine when thinking about yoga. As I played my edge, investigating how the fascia, meridians, chakras, and organs were all connected within our bodies, I learned to have patience and gentleness with myself as I faced the residual emotional, mental, and physical blockages within me. Through a regular and consistent practice of Yin Yoga, I was feeling better, healing from the inside out and loving the energy and freedom I experienced as I started to balance the light and dark inside me.

Freedom

To celebrate my newfound freedom and turning forty-years-old, I jumped out of an airplane. I was free like a bird flying through the sky where the clouds live, free falling toward the earth below, adrenaline pumping, wind whooshing against my body with a permanent grin across my face. And for the first time in a long time – it was a real smile, full of happiness. I didn't want it to end, but alas, the instructor I was tethered to deployed the parachute and I experienced a moment of bearable queasiness and sinus pressure. As we slowly floated in the air, I was once again in the space between the moments of life having an aerial view of my reality. In that surreal moment of true freedom after surviving my past, I knew I was going to thrive in the life I was creating. I was getting out of my comfort zone, breaking free of the box I had put myself in, and surrendering to a higher power. I felt hopeful and had faith in the new path that was forging ahead.

Yet, with the new adventure, freedom, and happiness, I would still find myself frustrated and stuck in the momentum of my past. I hit the restart button when I left my marriage. Yet, I still had old beliefs circling my mind with thoughts that I'd be alone forever. I believed that no one would ever love me, and my biggest fear was finding myself in a similar situation or falling into patterns of that older version of myself. Even with all of those old stories, I took a chance at dating.

Eventually, I found myself in love with a man named Brian, someone that I had known in my younger years and who had been supportive during the first year and a half I was back at home. There was a sense of safety and softness to him that the girls and I quickly warmed up to.

Navigating through a new relationship was exhilarating, and, with a long friendship behind us, we took the next step and rented a home together. Life was moving rapidly, and I was showing up for myself and doing the work to succeed in all aspects of my life. Within weeks of our move, I progressed into a recruiter position and, five short months later, advanced into management right before the start of a global pandemic.

With a *dis-ease* lingering among the masses, and the honeymoon phase waning, triggers were in full throttle. There was this underlying sense of discomfort like a splinter under the skin.

Shadow Work

I began a journey to understand my attraction to stress and how my response patterns were stuck in a hypervigilant and reactive state. To advance this process, I applied for a scholarship to a trauma-sensitive yoga program and was honored to be awarded a spot in the class. The training was supposed to be in-person but turned into the first of many Zoom sessions, leading me to complete the full 100-hour teacher training certification program within five months, one of the greatest perks of the pandemic and also the darkest part of my healing.

As I immersed myself in the program, I was invited to create a sense of inquiry and curiosity to investigate and experiment moving my body in different ways. As I followed the slower, rhythmic patterns into each pose, I felt more connected to myself. The yoga and breathwork I was experiencing kept me in the present moment, improving my nervous system while nourishing my soul instead of being forced to relive the past. During the online sessions, we dove into the polyvagal theory to understand the body's response to stress and how the vagus nerve connects from the brain to the colon and regulates our heart, breath, and even our appetites. We looked at fight, flight, freeze, and fawn responses to trauma, all of which I had experienced throughout my previous marriage. I recognized I was continuing to repeat some of these same exact patterns. I discovered that the plethora of undiagnosed health issues I experienced were actually trauma responses. Although there was no longer a threat to my overall wellbeing, my body had remained in a state of prolonged stress and anxiety, and I was unable to regulate my emotional responses in a healthy manner.

Even the phrase "calm down" set off a whirlwind of emotions as Brian said those two words to me when we were experiencing a minor frustration installing a headboard together. I tried to play it off since logically the scenario wouldn't be an issue for most people, but I was on the brink of tears and felt my chest cave in after those two words left Brian's lips. I dashed out of the room and my breathing was heavier when I fled to the kitchen. I felt the contents of my stomach rising up and stormed outside into the cool fresh air. Sobbing uncontrollably and gasping for air, I began to hyperventilate. Fear and confusion crept in, my heart pumping fast in my chest, face tingling and lightheaded, I wanted to escape and numb the pain, but I caught myself... *What the hell are you doing?* I slowly began catching my breath. My thoughts were forming again, and I felt the urge to walk barefoot in the grass. Feeling the damp refreshing blades of grass beneath the soles of my feet and slip in between my toes, I looked up toward the moon and stars in the night sky and swallowed a long, deep breath of air, filling up my chest and abdomen, and slowly released it all, sensing the warmth caressing my tongue as the air flowed through my mouth. With my breath normalizing, I went back inside, sipped a drink of water, wiped the tears off my face, and thanked Brian for allowing me to have this space. We embraced, tightly squeezing each other, and I felt the comfort that I had dreamed of for so long.

Through my work with trauma-informed yoga, I realized "calm down" activated a memory within my body that had me reacting as though I was living in my toxic past. My response to the trigger was not rational, but since Brian had taken the time to listen to what I was learning and experiencing, he provided the safe space and patience that I needed. I could see growth within me. If the scenario happened six months earlier, the reaction would have been different and ultimately led to a spiraling of unwanted events. I was determined to heal myself to be the best version of me so I could show up for the people that love me.

I continued my studies on trauma, reading multiple books and digging deep through the layers that I pulled over myself. I discovered there were many different parts of me, Internal Family Systems, each handling life in their own way with their own triggers, and some provided protection to the different parts while others were saboteurs. I had to examine and communicate with each part and work through the conflicts of my psyche to rewire my brain to create a better self. At the same time, my yoga practice evolved as I developed my own trauma-informed Yin Yoga. I found advancement while doing the slowest movements and slightest adjustments and enjoyed the predictability and control of my own self-practice.

It was my body, my yoga.

The rhythmic movements I was granted permission to explore in the trauma-sensitive yoga program helped me ease into the stillness of a Yin Yoga pose at my own pace. The most miniscule movements would lead to a crunch, tingle, whoosh in the side of my neck or a zing, pop, and release in the hip, opening up the channels in my body like water rushing through a collapsed dam. Both my inner and outer worlds were feeling lighter and freer with each alteration of my body. I was developing a new narrative, yet still had another hurdle to jump.

Metamorphosis

Being in limbo is a feeling deep below the surface that insidiously gnaws at you without being able to define it when you're stuck there. Most of my adult life I felt trapped in my chrysalis waiting for the right moment to spread my wings and have the freedom to fly. I never planned on falling in love again. I was afraid that if I surrendered and fully committed to someone, my past would repeat, and I would be back to square one in a life I felt stranded in. The truth is, although I fell in love with another man

– it was only made possible because I fell in love with myself.

It was now time to trust life (and myself) once again. So, I made the decision to fully commit to my new life with Brian and purchase a home together to establish our roots. This man respects me, supports me, and makes me happy, so it was time to get over my fear of the unknown.

I was no longer putting my life or happiness on hold; that was clear on move-in day when I brought in the final box of items from our temporary home to the place where we would spend the rest of our lives together. We were finally home, and I felt it in my soul.

As I look back, I feel immense appreciation for the transformation that has occurred in my life. I have intentionally created a life with purpose. I am proud of who I am becoming. I have a voice and a light that shines brightly. I am surrounded by friends, family, colleagues, and a new community of like-minded souls. I have faith that the universe will continue to manifest my dreams beyond anything I could ever imagine.

I am grateful for it all - my past, present, and future and thankful for every great spiritual teacher in my life. Today, I smile with peace, love, and happiness deep in my soul because I am unshackled and free to live life to my fullest potential.

Danielle

Danielle Hunter, a mother of two from Northeast Ohio, is a human resources manager at a non-profit dedicated to empowering individuals with intellectual and developmental disabilities. Her commitment to her community shines through her active roles on the boards of her local chamber of commerce and HR chapter. Danielle earned a Bachelor of Arts in English & Communication, minor in Writing, and she is a Society for Human Resource Management Certified Professional.

From a young age, Danielle embraced her creative spirit, engaging in art projects, writing, and sharing her passions with others. She turned to meditation during her early years of motherhood, practicing breathing exercises alongside her daughter to foster a tranquil bedtime routine. Her self-taught yoga journey began with library books and VHS tapes, laying the foundation for her practice well before stepping into a yoga studio.

Danielle's path to personal healing led her to become a trauma-informed Yin Yoga teacher and a Reiki Level Two practitioner. With these skills, she guides others toward their own healing, sharing the transformative power of mindful movement and energy work.

How to connect with Danielle:
Email: daniellehryogi@gmail.com
Link: https://linktr.ee/thehryogi

Narration on Danielle
with Cortney

Your life is what you say it is

As the early morning light filtered in through the half-open blinds of my bedroom window, I opened my eyes and realized it was a new day. I instantly popped up, excited and eager. There were butterflies in my stomach and a sense of anxiousness. Not the kind that brings you anxiety, but the kind where you are anticipating something exciting that is going to happen that day. There wasn't anything particularly special about this morning from the dozens before it. In truth, this is how I wake up most days – excited and eager.

Usually, I am up by 6:00am and in my office at my desk by 7:00am. Some days I spend 10+ hours in that office. Most people might read this and think, "That doesn't sound fun or exciting." But for me, I am living the life I have intentionally created. This is often what I choose to do. Some days I'm in front of a group of people teaching and sharing my story. Other days I sit for hours, with my bare feet in the grass, watching the dragonflies dance along the pond's edge as I dream up what I will do next. I have created a life where I can choose what my day will look like.

This wasn't always the case. I used to live life similar to most – wake up to my alarm, go to work, come home, sit on the couch, watch TV, go to bed. Wake up to my alarm, go to work, come home, sit on the couch, watch TV, go to bed. Wake up to my alarm, go to work, come home, sit on the couch, watch TV, go to bed. Wait for the weekend. Drink on Friday night. Sleep in on Saturday morning. On Sunday, feel the dread of Monday looming where I would do it all over again - wake up to my alarm, go to work, come home, sit on the couch, watch TV, go to bed. If you think this is a dreamy scenario, good for you – that's awesome. For me, it wasn't terrible. I didn't hate it. But I certainly didn't pop out of bed every morning, without an alarm clock, eager for the day. I was just going through the motions.

One day, I went to work and there was a "Lunch and Learn" workshop where we were going to talk about a new documentary called *The Secret* – maybe you've heard of it.

This was twenty years ago when the concept of the "law of attraction" truly was a secret to most. During the lunch and learn series we would explore one chapter of *The Secret* each week, for twelve weeks. I remember raising my hand at the end of the first session and saying, "Is that it? What's the secret?" I guess I was hoping for more. Little did I know my life was never going to be the same.

Although I was not impressed (yet), something nagged at me, and I went home that day and watched the full documentary on my own. After it was over, I sat there in awe. This was the first time anyone had ever explained to me that I was actually the creator of my own life. It's hard for me to articulate, but, up until that point, I really thought life was just happening to me. I didn't realize I had control. In the documentary, Neal Donald Walsch (who I soon became obsessed with and read every word he ever published) said, *"There is no blackboard in the sky on which God has written your purpose, your mission in life. So, your purpose is what you say it is. Your mission is the mission you give yourself. Your life will be what you create it as, and no one will stand in judgment of it, now or ever."*

I will never forget how I felt in that moment.
Freedom.

That was the beginning of me creating my own life on my own terms.
I never looked back.

If you are living a life that you did not create on purpose, I want you to know you have the power to change it. In fact, YOU are the only one with the power to change it.

For some of you that is exciting. For others you might be thinking, "Oh crap – it's all up to me?"

Maybe this is a foreign concept to you, like it was to me before watching *The Secret*. Or maybe you've heard this concept before, but it hasn't really taken residence in your subconscious. Until that happens, you're not really believing it, so it can't become your truth.

As you read through the rest of this book, you are going to hear from people who have absolutely created their own life, on their own terms, regardless of what someone else told them. I hope it inspires you to create yours – by design – not by default.

WESLEY
The Man Behind the Adventure

Wesley

The Man Behind the Adventure

Cortney: Do you know why I wanted to interview you for this book?

Wesley: I'm guessing because I am a time traveler.

Cortney: (Chuckling) – Yes, perhaps that is part of the reason. It's not so much that you are a time traveler as that you left us with many mysteries and questions with both of your chapters in the books *Stories of Alchemy* and *Epiphany*.

Wesley: Mysteries and questions, yes, I guess I did.

Cortney: In fact, I get asked all the time about you. People first ask me, "Is this for real?" and then they ask me: How did we meet? Do I know you? Have we ever met in person? Will Wesley be writing a book? Overall, they are just very interested in you and the life you've lived. To provide context for those who haven't read your other chapters, in *Stories of Alchemy*, you claim to be a time traveler and in *Epiphany* you tell a story about a near death experience that you had when you were 11 years old. Correct?

Wesley: Yes, that is correct. I can travel back in time. Today, at the ripe age of 44, I rarely do that anymore. But, yes, I have traveled to the past hundreds, if not thousands of times.

Cortney: Have you ever traveled to the future?

Wesley: No, that is not something I can do, only to the past.

Cortney: Ok, interesting, I don't think I realized that from your other stories.

Wesley: There are so many things that are not included in those stories I've told with you, with just a couple of thousand words. I feel like my life could fill thousands of chapters.

Cortney: Yes, I would agree. And I would like to get to more of that, but first – I'd love to answer the most common questions I get asked about you - How did we meet? Do I know you? Have I seen you in person? Do you want to share how we met?

Wesley: Yes, of course. I was on a Podcast website – it's like a matchmaking site for podcasts – almost like swipe left if you are interested in being on my podcast, swipe right if you aren't. I saw an ad promoting your book *Stories of Alchemy*. You were looking for authors. I had never shared my story publicly in any form and when I saw the title of the book and its premise, I was instantly intrigued with the idea that I could share what I have learned about being a time traveler with the world without revealing my identity.

Cortney: What do you think intrigued you so much about the book?

Wesley: I still think about that to this day. It was odd because I never had any desire to share my story publicly before. As soon as I saw the ad and the book title, I knew I was supposed to contact you and write a chapter in the book.

Cortney: This is interesting because you've never told me this before.

Wesley: The concept of pain to purpose was intriguing to me. My greatest pain was losing my dad back in 2013 and it never occurred to me that there was some kind of "purpose" to the pain. I instantly knew I had to share what I learned from my dad – particularly what he shared with me right before his passing. It was my dad communicating with me through your ad. He was telling me to share it with the world.

Cortney: Ah! Things are starting to make more sense to me now because I had never been on that podcast website before and never used it again. I was led there one day by one of my team members. I created that post about looking for authors and then never went on the website again. Now, I know why. It was your dad! So, we've never met in person, but we have talked on the phone many times.

Wesley: Yes, that is correct. My identity, for obvious reasons, must remain a mystery.

Cortney: So, you write your stories under the name Wesley, but that is not your real name.

Wesley: Correct, my name is not Wesley.

Cortney: Do you mind if I ask you why you use the name Wesley.

Wesley: When I turned 18, the movie *Blade* came out with Wesley Snipes. Let's just say ever since then he has become my mentor.

Cortney: Ok, we will leave it at that and jump into some of the burning questions I have.

Wesley: Sounds good. Let's go.

Cortney: In *Stories of Alchemy*, you say that your dad encouraged you to use this gift of time travel for what he called the "big important stuff in life." Not for fame, fortune, or material success such as acquiring money. But you didn't listen to this advice when he first told you at the age of 18. Instead, you spent most of your younger years acquiring just that – wealth, fame, and fortune. It wasn't until your dad became terminally ill in 2012, when you were in your thirties, that you began to understand what he was trying to tell you when you were 18. What was it that he was trying to tell you? What was it that he wanted you to share in *Stories of Alchemy*?

Wesley: I learned two big things from my dad passing. Up until that point, I looked at most of life as mundane. I lived from one big adventure to the next. I craved excitement. The moments in between the big adventures were meaningless and, quite frankly, boring to me. I did not see value in those moments. After my dad passed, I realized that the moments in between were **the moments**. I've lived a very "exciting" life by many people's standards, and I can tell you that the "mundane" moments are the ones I live for now.

Cortney: What do you mean by you've lived an "exciting" life?

Wesley: From the ages of 18 to 32, I rubbed elbows with the rich and the famous. I've built empires. I've partied with presidents. I've been mentored by the greatest men and women alive. I've been around the world, literally multiple times, including to space. I've seen and done it all in the name of adventure.

Cortney: Ok, well that's hard for a "normal" person like me to even understand.

Wesley: But that is kind of the point I am making here. None of that compares to what I realized after my dad died - that life was really about the "mundane" moments in life.

Cortney: Can you give me an example of what you are calling the "mundane" moments?

Wesley: Slowing down and paying attention to the synchronicities of life. When I was living for adventure and excitement, I missed all the signs that God was trying to give me. The signs that were taking me on the "real adventure" that I had signed up for before coming to this body on earth. For example, seeing that ad and knowing I had to contact you. Not knowing why, or where it would lead, but knowing that my dad was guiding me towards you.

Cortney: So, you were following what I like to call the breadcrumbs.

Wesley: Yes, exactly. Trusting that there are breadcrumbs being left for you. You can't see the breadcrumbs unless you are slowing down to the pace of life, living in the moments in between the bigger moments.

Cortney: You said you learned two big things from your dad's passing. What is the second thing you've learned?

Wesley: There was nothing in life to go back to and change. I realized this after my year of "second takes."

Cortney: Tell those who didn't read *Stories of Alchemy* what you mean by second takes.

Wesley: That's what my dad called going back and living your day a second time.

Cortney: You are referring to time travel here?

Wesley: Yes, my dad told me, each day, live your life just as any other ordinary human. Which meant, live your life and engage in what the day brought you. Then, with your gift of time travel, go back and live each day a second time. But this second time, instead of living life stressed or with thoughts of worry and driven by tasks, simply enjoy each moment.

Cortney: And you did this?

Wesley: Yes, I did this every day for a year. Before my dad passed, I never relived a full day before. I would only time travel to re-enjoy something I deemed spectacular or to fix things from the past.

Cortney: To fix things?

Wesley: Yes, if it didn't turn out the way I liked the first time, I would go back and fix it.

Cortney: Ok, wow!

Wesley: I know, sounds crazy right? But that is where the second biggest learning came in. I realized after the year of second takes that there were no problems that needed to be fixed. I realized that everything was working out perfectly for me. When I would go back and try to fix things, I was actually ruining the perfect unfolding. I began to trust, however awful a situation appeared in the moment, that with time and perspective, everything was happening by a divine plan. And I am not talking about someone else's divine plan, but my own divine plan. Again, back to the breadcrumbs. I like that term; I am going to use it now. The breadcrumbs are being left by you. You are guiding you.

Cortney: Ok, so that leads me to a question I often like to ask people who have spent time exploring what I will call spirituality. What do you know for sure?

Wesley: Is that an Oprah question?

Cortney: I guess, yes, it is...

Wesley: There are two things that I know for sure after my near-death experience (NDE) that I talk about in the book *Epiphany*. First, I know the woman who comforted me with the lullaby during my NDE was not a figment of my imagination. Since then, many of the things she shared with me that day have come true. I think the veil between our two worlds is very thin. For those who have a desire and a belief, I think you can access both worlds. However, for most of us, I don't think that is why we are here. I think a few are selected so that they can give hope and reassurance to others, but that is not the bigger intention.

Cortney: What do you mean when you say that is not why we are here? Can you expand on that?

Wesley: I realize that my life seems impossible. Probably even made-up. And that's probably why I have never shared it publicly until recently. I am not on a mission to convince people about time travel or near-death experiences. Quite the opposite, in fact. What I am trying to do with my story is convince people that escaping life, whether with time travel or a near-death experience, is not what we came here to do. I know it probably seems glamorous or special in some way, but what I've been able to glean from my admittedly unique life is that I see people trying to escape their lives – as if there is more. There isn't "more." There is only this moment. Where we came from is magnificent, magical, unearthly, unbinding, unlimited, no space, no time – our minds can't process our eternalness. And our eternalness decided to come here and BE earthly, binding, limited, tied to space and time for a reason. I think the reason is different for every single person. What I meant when I said 'that is not why we are here' is that trying to leave the moment is the exact opposite of what we came here to do. And that is the story I am trying to tell. Not the story about time travel or death. It's about life. In this moment.

Cortney: I just heard that in a new way for the very first time. We came here to be earthly, binding, limited. Wow. And what is the second thing that you know for sure?

Wesley: Well, I kind of just alluded to it. We are both temporary and eternal at the same time. We are not what we seem. When I had my near-death experience and rose above my body, I realized I was not that boy, not that body. I was something so much more. It's a paradox that I still continue to piece together as an adult. Although, as I just mentioned, I don't think I am supposed to piece it together. Nor that I could ever really understand it fully.

Cortney: Absolutely brilliant. I have chills running down my arms. Wow!

Wesley: And that is the greatest gift of this life – having a human body to experience those chills. Right?!

Cortney: Is it ok if I ask you a series of rapid-fire questions now? Just answer quickly with the first thing that comes to your mind.

Wesley: Yes, of course. This will be fun!

Cortney: What continues to drive you?

Wesley: Now, it's my children. I hope to be half the father my father was to me.

Cortney: What strengths or unique things about your personality do you think have contributed to your success?

Wesley: Ha, that's funny, I guess you would expect me to say my time-traveling. However, I am going to surprise you and say my love of adventure has been the true spark to my success. I will try anything once. I am not afraid to try new things. I am not afraid to fail. I live outside my comfort zone and always have even as a young child.

Cortney: What do you think every visionary or trailblazer must possess?

Wesley: Gumption to begin; charisma must follow.

Cortney: What would we be surprised to know about you?

Wesley: I only have nine toes.

Cortney: What would we be surprised to know about you in a business context?

Wesley: That even now, with an unimaginable amount of worldly success, I often feel like an imposter.

Cortney: Really? Why?

Wesley: I have thought about this a lot. It's the fact that I have a safety net that most people don't have. I tell myself that is the only reason why I have reached such heights of success.

Cortney: When you say safety net, you mean...

Wesley: Time travel. I can literally go back and change things. And I have. But besides that, I think me, in this body, feels like an imposter, because I am a fraction of who I really am beyond this body. Going back to what I said earlier about trying to piece together my impermanence and eternalness.

Cortney: And that makes you an imposter?

Wesley: I'm just acknowledging that I know some of the most successful people in the world and, on some days, they all feel like imposters.

Cortney: Agreed. This is interesting to know. Now, back to the rapidfire questions – if that's ok. What do you lie awake thinking about at night?

Wesley: I sleep like a baby.

Cortney: How many people who know you, know you are a time traveler?

Wesley: One, and he's dead.

Cortney: Who is your favorite "famous" person?

Wesley: Wow, that is hard to pick just one. I'll say Eddie Murphy.

Cortney: You said earlier that you have traveled the world multiple times, where is your favorite place to go?

Wesley: Aside from my hometown in New Zealand – I love visiting Bali.

Cortney: Dogs or cats?

Wesley: Does it have to be a dog or cat? I think zebras are the most magnificent creatures alive.

Cortney: Favorite food?

Wesley: Tom yum goong in a small restaurant just outside of Bangkok.

Cortney: Favorite show or movie?

Wesley: *Blade* – again, Wesley Snipes. I also love the show *How I Met Your Mother* – laughing is the best medicine. I never understood why people watch shows that make them anxious or scared, there's already enough anxiety and fear in 'real' life.

Cortney: Ok, one last question. The question I get asked the most about you. Who was the woman in the boat? The woman you talk about in the book *Epiphany*.

Wesley: Do you really want me to share that answer with you now?

Cortney: Umm, yes! I totally want to know. I am dying to know.

Wesley: The woman in the boat is my wife's mother.

Cortney: What? Your wife's mother?

Wesley: Yes. And that story will blow your mind too.

Cortney: Ok, everyone is going to kill me for saying this, but let's hold on to that story for another time. Will you share that story with us – perhaps in your own book?

Wesley: Yes. You and I have talked about that a couple of times, and I would love to write my own book. Maybe one day that will actually happen.

Cortney: Yes. I have no doubt that one day it will.
Thank you for sharing more of your story and thoughts with us for this book.

Wesley: Thank you for giving me the avenue to share. I appreciate it more than you will ever know. And a big thanks to Dad for that.

Cortney: Yes, indeed, your dad is no doubt the driving force for all of these stories and hopefully more.
Until next time!

Wesley

Wesley shares this story under a pen name.

Wesley is happily married to his soul-mate. They have two beautiful daughters together. Wesley was born in a small town called Glenorchy in New Zealand and moved to the United States at the age of sixteen. Wesley spent almost 15 years amassing fortune and fame before settling down and living a simpler life as a husband and a father. Wesley is a successful trailblazer and visionary who has started over a dozen companies that have made millions of dollars.

Wesley's writings can also be found in the books *Stories of Alchemy* and *Epiphany*.

How to connect with Wesley:
Communication for Wesley can be sent via SHINE Ohio to cortney@shineohio.com

MARYANNE PETKAC
Test My Limits or Play it Safe?

Maryanne

Test My Limits or Play it Safe?

I ran my first full marathon at the ripe old age of 49 in May 2008 (The Flying Pig in Cincinnati, OH). Two weeks later, I graduated from university with my Bachelor of Arts in English. On August 30, 2008, I ran my second full marathon (Pocatello Marathon in Pocatello, ID). Six days later, on September 5, 2008, I turned 50 years old.

I am sharing this information in the hopes of inspiring someone, maybe YOU, who has been feeling the itch to run, who has been wondering if you've got what it takes, to push beyond your limits, and to feel the euphoria and pride when you cross the finish line NO MATTER HOW LONG THE RACE DISTANCE. In the process, I discovered the strength, determination, and drive that was hidden deep within myself and the belief that I can accomplish anything I set my mind to! Maybe you can, too!

I never was a runner, at least not in the popular sense. Hell, I wasn't even what some would consider an athlete. I grew up in a small town where friends, the library, pool, and rec center were all within walking distance, so my friends and I walked everywhere. I took swimming lessons at the local pool. We all did. After failing miserably at a local swim show and seeing my parents' disappointment, I carried within me the belief that I didn't have what it took to be an athlete. Curiously, it never crossed my mind to ask about additional activities where I might have excelled.

I went to an all-girls high school where the focus wasn't on sports, but rather on teaching young women how to be good secretaries in the business world. Yes, this was a thing back in the 1970s. Upon graduation, I worked downtown and got my cardio from walking to the bus stop (1/4 mile away), from the train station to my office building (7/10 mile), then reversing my steps each evening. I joined a gym where I strength trained. After getting married and having a family in my late twenties/early thirties, my primary cardio (once my sons were too big for stroller walks) came from walking my yellow lab, Murphy, around our neighborhood. It wasn't until I began working in the emergency room of a local hospital and saw patients coming in with chest pains and heart attacks that I began to seriously look into ramping up my cardiovascular fitness. Working with physicians gave me access to many sources of information about the best way to increase cardiac endurance, and running, obviously, was an option that I considered.

I began walking Murphy past a few houses up the street, breaking into a slow run past a few more houses, then dropping back to a walk. This rhythm continued up and down our neighborhood streets. As my endurance built, I was able to run a little farther. At the time, I had no plan, no schedule, and no race in my future. I wasn't even aware that such opportunities existed. I guess I was just testing myself to see if I could do it. At the time, I was raising three young sons, working full-time, and going to a local community college a few nights a week. I didn't receive any support or encouragement from my first husband. I remember hanging my report cards on our refrigerator door, but he never acknowledged the accomplishments of my good grades. Ironically, when I had the support from my parents, I wasn't able to excel at swimming. Now, I had no encouragement from my husband, but I was excelling in school.

Soon, my life changed in a way that allowed me to look for new opportunities, entertain them as real possibilities, and break free from the boundaries that were holding me back.

In 2004, I remarried. My husband, Joe, was a runner throughout grade school and high school; running both track and cross country in high school. After taking a break from competing, but still running for enjoyment, Joe started running in local marathons. He completed his first in 1993.

When we started dating, Joe would tell me about the marathons he ran (over 100 road races at that time). He'd talk about the races with excitement, always sharing his finish time and whether he had negative splits (which meant nothing to me back then). I started going to some of Joe's marathons, but I'd meet him on the racecourse since the start time was usually around 7am, which was way too early to be dressed, have breakfast, drive, and park at the event. Luckily, Joe had run enough races to loosely determine what mile-marker he'd be near at a specific time, so I could stand on the racecourse and wait for him to run by. People were cheering, clanging cowbells, waving signs, and volunteering at aid stations where water was offered in little paper cups along with energy gel packs. Of course, watching a race is quite different from actively participating in one. Once Joe ran by, I could try to navigate through city blocks to find him as he passed another mile marker, meet him at the finish line (which could be another hour or so), or just pack up and go home. Waiting at the finish line had its merits.

Watching runners cross the finish line is almost as exciting as being at the marathon expo. Some people cry, some are overcome with laughter, some fall to their knees and kiss the ground, some hug whomever is there for them. It was quite exhilarating to hear the announcer call out Joe's name as he crossed the finish line. As the runner, you often don't hear your name being called. At the finish line, there are lots of smiles, high-fives, hugs, shouts, and tears. It's an accomplishment that fewer than one percent of the population ever tries.

The race expo is held the day before the marathon. They are usually held in a convention center to support the massive crowds. Runners come to the expo to pick up their bib numbers and their race t-shirt. Race t-shirts are usually not worn on the day of the actual race but after the race has been successfully finished; it's considered by some to be a bad omen to wear it on race day (something to which I've always subscribed). Runners receive their swag bags and shop hundreds of vendors who come to sell their merch (everything from clothing to shoes to massages).

The excitement at the expos is palpable. The event is buzzing with chatter as runners greet each other, walk from vendor to vendor to see what may give them an edge the next day, talk about their plans for dinner that evening, or maybe register for an up-and-coming advertised race. The expos are brimming with laughter, nerves, excitement, and camaraderie. Walking into the expo and seeing runners who have already picked up their swag bags brings the anticipation to an all-time high.

After accompanying Joe to many of these expos, I started to realize that my preconceived notions of what a runner looked like were not accurate. I observed at the expos and races that not all runners are built the same; they come in all shapes and sizes. Their confidence doesn't come from how they look on the outside, but from the belief in themselves that they carry within. It's the confidence that they've trained enough for the task at hand; that they've put the miles in to successfully cross that finish line and proudly wear the finisher medal that's placed around their neck.

I found myself wanting to be a part of the running crowd – as a runner. I wanted to experience the excitement and the possibility – as a runner. I wanted to move from the sidelines to be part of the race – to test and stretch my limits; to see what I was made of; to push past all the beliefs that I held about myself; and to see what I could accomplish. With the unconditional support of my husband, I knew that I could run a marathon. I was unstoppable.

I asked Joe if he thought I could run. He said, "Yes." I asked him if he thought I could run a 5K (3.1 miles). He again answered, "Yes." So, it was settled; I'd begin training for a 5K. We researched local 5Ks in our area and found one held in the memory of a local woman who had recently passed. Running in someone's memory was a wonderful impetus.

I began training in the evening, after work, on the outdoor track at the local high school. Joe coached me to run once around the track, which is equivalent to 1/4 mile. Once I was able to run 1/4 mile non-stop, I ran 1/2 mile, slowly progressing to 3/4, before facing the ultimate challenge— an entire mile, or 4 times around the track.

I found it difficult to break my first mile, and it took me several attempts. I think most of that was self-sabotage; I didn't really believe that I could do it. It seemed like such a monumental challenge. There is an adage that all runners believe to be true: running is 90% mental and only 10% physical. Joe sat on the bleachers and offered encouragement, but I knew I had to do the work. Eventually, I told myself that I could "do this" and finally broke one mile. I was immediately filled with so much pride that I had mastered what I had once seen as an impossible obstacle. Being able to run that first mile non-stop proved to me that I could do anything I set my mind to.

I ran my first 5K in March 2007. My official finish time was 31:25 (31 minutes, 25 seconds). Not the fastest time, but I felt incredible.

I did it! I was a runner!

My proud husband met me at the finish with tears in his eyes. I couldn't wait to run another race! So that's what I did.

I registered for the May 2007 Rite Aid Cleveland Marathon/Half Marathon 10K (6.2 miles). I was ecstatic when I crossed the finish line in 1:04:40! My husband was running the marathon and unable to share in my victory at that moment, so I called my then 79-year-old father and told him the exciting news. It was a far cry from a marathon, but I knew I was on my way to running 26.2 miles.

Four months later, I challenged myself to run a half-marathon in Albuquerque, New Mexico. We arrived a few days early to adjust to the altitude. This was a smaller race without a lot of crowd support, but it allowed us the opportunity to run on mostly empty roads past the gorgeous Sandia Mountains and to revel in the understated beauty of the southwest. Finishing that race (in 2:26:33) made me realize that although I wasn't the fastest runner, I was determined to finish and add another endorsement to my previously questionable level of self-confidence. I was ready to register for a full-fledged marathon. So that's what I did.

In January 2008, Joe and I decided to run the Flying Pig Marathon in Cincinnati in May of that year. I had a lot going on that spring. Aside from working full-time and having three sons living at home, I was set to graduate with my Bachelor of Arts degree two weeks after the marathon, so there were papers to write and presentations to give. The weather doesn't care about or cooperate with spring marathoners in training. Joe and I would run after work through our neighborhood in the dark and in the snow. It's important to be consistent when running these short runs, so we'd run three miles each evening, taking one rest day for recovery.

Weekends are for long runs. These runs are not for the faint of heart. They build each weekend. So, if a long run is six miles one weekend day, it'll be eight the next, and so on, gradually maxing out at about 20 miles. The thought is that adrenalin, endorphins, and the crowds at the race will push any runner through from mile 20 to across the finish line.

I will confess to not being a fan of long runs. Intellectually, I know they're needed to provide the framework I required to rely upon on race day. Long runs built my physical strength, tolerance, and mental resilience. They gave me the satisfaction of running many miles and the encouragement that I needed to run more. Due to the uncooperative weather in NE Ohio January-March, I did most of my long runs on my basement treadmill. Yep, I would run for up to three hours, sometimes more, while watching some insipid Lifetime movie to keep my mind from focusing on my legs. It may have been a little unorthodox for experienced runners, but it worked for me.

When we initially registered in January for the Flying Pig Marathon, race day seemed so far away. All of a sudden, the time was here, and, as we drew nearer to race day, I started questioning what I was doing, and if I had the ability to finish a 26.2-mile race at the age of 49. Joe was reassuring, telling me that my training would take me across the finish line. It's easy to doubt yourself when the task at hand seems next to impossible, no matter how many miles you've put in to ensure a race finish. All I could do was trust in my training and believe that I could cross the finish line in one piece.

Joe and I arrived at the expo for our packet pick-up, and it was, as I remembered, brimming with people, excitement, music, and laughter. It was the first time that I was at an expo as a full marathon runner. I won't lie, it boosts your self-esteem a bit, like you're one of the "big dogs." We stood in line for our running bibs, then made our way over to the table with the race t-shirts and swag bags. Although I had always chided Joe about his collection of marathon posters, I found myself in possession of one and promised to frame it, as a nod to my first marathon. We walked around a bit, pausing at the many tables to talk to the vendors and sample different products.

I don't remember if I slept much the night before the race, but all of a sudden it was race day and time to get ready. Our race day breakfast consisted of a bagel, banana, and peanut butter. We met our friends in the lobby of the hotel and walked together to the starting line corral, joining thousands of other runners. It promised to be a beautiful day with sunshine and warm temps. This was not ideal for running a marathon, but at that point, I knew I needed to make the best of it.

Outside of the starting corral, there are usually tons of port-o-johns and no shortage of runners lined up to use them. I usually view port-o-johns as pretty gross, but today they were an absolute necessity for my nervous bladder.

Once the start of the race is signaled, the runners in the front of the corral take off. I was in the back and began to walk toward the starting line, making sure my running bib was registered by the chip timer. It can take 10 minutes to reach the chip timer, depending on the number of runners. My run time didn't start until I crossed the chip timer.

And then I was off. Joe ran with me for about a mile. Being a more seasoned and faster runner, he eventually took off. I watched his shirt fade into the distance and continued toward the finish line, 25 miles into the future.

In a marathon, or any other type of race, you're never alone. There are people, elbows, feet, discarded jackets, dropped water bottles, etc. on the road. It's worse after you reach an aid station; there are crumpled paper cups and torn empty gel packets littering the streets. Aid station volunteers try their best to rake the trip hazards out of the way of the runners. The volunteers are the greatest, and I would try to thank them whenever I could.

I ran the marathon course at a nice pace for about nine miles, then I slowed to a walk. Walking is not discouraged nor disgraced. In fact, there are some methods of marathon training that encourage walking for one minute and running nine throughout the entire race. I wasn't subscribing to this method, mainly because I hadn't heard of it yet. I just wanted to collect my thoughts and do a mental check-in. So, I walked some and ran some. At some point, there are no crowds, no music, and the runners/walkers are scattered ahead of and behind you. I was mainly by myself with my thoughts. Each mile marker, though, brings a sense of relief that I only had "X" number of miles to go. At one point, I was questioning my mental acuity, chastising myself and regretting the hours spent on the pavement towards my goal of 26.2 miles; hours I would never get back. I don't want to sugarcoat my time on the course. Mentally, I was pretty strong and determined to finish, but physically, well, that's another story.

You learn in training that you need to stay hydrated. I drank my body weight in water and hydration drinks, but I never felt the urge to use the port-o-johns; I simply didn't have to go. My swollen fingers looked like sausages, and I wondered if I'd ever be able to get my wedding ring off. I was sweating, probably due to a combination of the constant liquid intake and the temps, and, as a result, I had salt stains on my face. My dry-tech shirt was wet. I began to chafe. Suffice to say, for days I had rashes in places that were not visible to the public eye. But my drive to cross that finish line was strong so I kept on with relentless forward progress.

Eventually, I found myself at mile 23. It was here that I saw Joe walking toward me. He had already finished his marathon but came back to see where I was and to offer encouragement. "Only three more miles to go!" he exclaimed. If only I felt as happy as he sounded. But I knew I had it in me to finish those three miles.

The closer you get to the end of a marathon, the more the landscape changes. The crowds are back, cheering and waving upbeat signs, the bands are playing motivational songs, and you can hear the announcer calling the names of the runners as they cross the finish line. It pumps you up and gives you the momentum to finish.

When I finally reached the finish line, Joe stepped aside so I could cross it by myself. I was sweaty, stinky, starving, and deliriously proud of myself as a finisher medal was placed around my neck. I had tears in my eyes as I realized my dream of running and finishing a marathon. It's an almost indescribable feeling of happiness, pride, and pure unadulterated joy. The race photographer did his best to capture my feelings in the finish line photo. I had done what I had set out to do: at the ripe old age of 49, I ran my first marathon. And two weeks later, I graduated cum laude with my BA.

I had two questions, though. When was the next marathon and how soon could I register?

At the time of writing this chapter, I have completed seven full marathons and several more half-marathons. In 2012, I began to explore trail running and completed a trail ultra (50K or 31 miles) in 2013. At the age of 66, I continue to push myself to explore new life-giving experiences. I realize that I can test my limits or play it safe, and you can, too.

Sincerely,
Maryanne

Maryanne's collection of medals from her races

Maryanne

Maryanne Petkac lives in Northeast Ohio with her husband. They have five adult children and six grandchildren at the time of this writing.

After years of being a daily wine drinker, Maryanne decided to put her health first and quit drinking in March 2019. Now, Maryanne is a certified This Naked Mind coach. She uses science and compassion to help individuals who want to stop using alcohol and need assistance throughout the process.

Maryanne discovered yoga in 1997. In May 2021, she became a Registered Yoga Instructor (RYT-200) through the Cleveland Clinic School of Yoga. She teaches adaptive yoga, trauma-informed meditation, and mindfulness practices to the military community and first responders.

She is a marathoner and a trail runner who loves to inspire others with her story.

How to connect with Maryanne:
Website: sobersunrisescoaching.com
Email: mpetkac08@jcu.edu
Instagram: maryannepetkaccoaching

Narration on Maryanne
with Cortney

Age is just a story

It's February 2024 and, after two and a half years of perimenopause, I am now - by definition - in menopause after not having a cycle for 12 full months. The joys of knowing that I am done with having a period are short-lived as almost instantly my physical body begins to show signs of all the awful stories I've heard others share about their menopausal experience.

It felt like overnight I went from having a flat tummy to having a protruding stomach. I gained ten pounds in less than two months, after trying incessantly to lose weight. I was having trouble sleeping at night because of the hot flashes. I struggled to stay awake, succumbing to taking naps in the afternoon, just to make it through the day. When I was awake, I could not focus. My memory was failing me.

For two months, I felt so sorry for myself as the momentum was beginning to build. I even noticed that I was attracting other people telling me about their horror stories around menopause even though I wasn't starting the conversation. It didn't matter, the Universe was matching me up with people of the same frequency.

After two months, I woke up one day (finally) and decided this wasn't going to be my experience anymore. I've spent years telling people how to deliberately create their lives and here I was falling into a similar trap of letting external factors dictate my life. I knew better than anyone how to stop this runaway train.

I had to change my mindset.

I had a friend tell me, "Everyone gets to be young, but not everyone gets to be old."

That was the turning point. I started searching for people who were thriving in menopause. I let that become my dominate intent as I deliberately sought out those telling a story I wanted to mirror in my life. I was inspired by women in the best shape of their lives at the age of fifty. Women who were happy and healthy. I decided I wasn't going to succumb to what mass consciousness thought about menopause, instead, I would tell my own story. I read about how other cultures have very different experiences – they relish and thrive in these years; they are more creative, wiser, and more revered. They start to fully live into their purpose at this age and feel more freedom and love. I decided that would be my story too.

Within a few days, I was feeling better. I had shifted the momentum and was now going in the right direction. Some people say age is just a number. I say age is just a story.

Shortly after that, I attracted a device into my life that changed everything.

I believe as I shifted my frequency about age, the Universe gave me the exact tool I needed.

By using this frequency device, within less than ten days, I was sleeping through the night; I lost 5 pounds; I had energy, focus, and stamina. My hormones were balanced, and I felt amazing.

Whether you decide to run a marathon or start a new career at the age of 49 – don't let your age discourage you. It's just a story. You can do anything at any age.

P.S. If you are wondering what frequency device I am talking about, click the QR code on the right to learn more.

KALYANNA (YANNA) WILLIAMS
Plot Twist

Kalyanna

Plot Twist

"My story is not one of triumph, but one of truth." -Yanna Williams

In this chapter, I take you through the vibrant narrative of my journey filled with personal growth, resilience, and the powerful realization of my true potential. You'll experience my heartfelt reflections and the inspiring moments that paint a picture of overcoming adversity and embracing my unique strengths. Prepare to be captivated by my raw and honest recounting of dreams, challenges, and triumphs, highlighting how I turned perceived disadvantages into my greatest advantages.

A Girl Can Dream

"They're ready for you in the conference room," my assistant said, breaking my gaze with a knock on the door. The team was set for our quarter close-out meeting. This is our largest meeting at the end of our fiscal year, right before we take a company-wide Rest and Recharge for the next two weeks. It's a beautiful summer day, the sun glistening over the water, gleaming with blues and greens outside my large office window. There are two more days left in the week, and I'm off to vacation with my entire family in Aruba. Five days with seventeen adults and twelve children. I laugh out loud, thinking about how crazy I am for providing an all-expenses-paid vacation for my entire family! The chaos and joy are sure to provide more stories than I'll have the capacity to share.

I take a deep breath, coming back to the moment and realizing that the team is still waiting for me. I grab my things from my desk and head to our conference room down the hall. I hear my heels clicking against the floor with every step in the empty, quiet hallway. As I approach the conference room, the open glass windows reveal the team talking and laughing together as they wait to start the meeting. Upon my entrance, we exchange greetings, and everyone takes their seats. My COO stands up, prepared to address the room.

"Hello, everyone, and welcome to our annual close-out meeting. We have been a very busy team this year, and we are grateful for the hard work and dedication of each and every one of you. We wouldn't be us without you, and we thank you. As we close out this fiscal year, I am proud to report that we have not only surpassed our goal but have more than doubled it! We have closed the year with $9,362,431.22."

Cheers, high-fives, hell yeahs, and applause fill the room. Our COO continues, "I am also proud to announce that... drumroll, please... we have secured the seven-figure contract from Maroon Enterprises!" More cheers and applause fill the room. The excitement is infectious as we celebrate together. I stand.

"Team, I can't be more proud to be the SHE-EO of this company. When I started this company, my goal was to have a team of the best and the brightest solving the most difficult business problems in the most innovative, disruptive way. I set forth for us to be trendsetters, changemakers, and, of course, make a whole lotta money! WE have done just that! I dreamed of this moment, and now..."

"Yanna! Yanna!" My husband wakes me up from my sleep. Yet, I am still dreaming of this moment.

My Two Disadvantages
"You were born with two disadvantages: you're Black and you're a woman." The piercing words from my aunt replay in my head as I look in the mirror, eyes pressed on my reflection. Black. Woman. Disadvantages. Words have always been important to me. From the time I could make sentences, reading has been my favorite hobby. I won all the awards for reading the most books, maxing out my library card every week, then needing to go back the next week for more. For me, reading was an adventure, my world outside of my actual world. Something about the way each author crafted their words so meticulously, evoking imagination and emotion in each sentence, resonated with me. Each character was real, entangled in their own narrative—adventurous, different, yet real. For me, words mattered. Black. Woman. Disadvantages. These words mattered. Yet, at that moment, with my aunt giving what she perceived as the biggest life lesson, the meaning of her words didn't resonate. My spirit rejected them. Instantly, I decided that being a Black woman would *not* be a disadvantage. I was going to write my own narrative and be a successful Black woman. And when I could, I would make sure no other aunt would ever have to warn her niece about her two disadvantages.

Reading My Diary Out Loud
I am originally from Chicago, Illinois. The North Lawndale area on the

west side, to be exact. I am proud of my roots, although our community typically has a bad name. Growing up, I was surrounded by family, friends, and a lot of love. My family on both sides is very close, always looking for a reason to get together and have fun. From sleepovers to cookouts, we do it all! And we do it all TOGETHER! What I observed very young, however, is that my dad's side of the family was much wealthier. They had nice cars, beautiful homes, went on extravagant vacations, and had great careers. I admired that. I wanted my life to look like that. I recall asking my aunt, "How did you get this house and this car?" She said, "Go to college, then get a great job and work hard." I wrote that down in my memory!

In March of 2010, I received my acceptance letter from Tuskegee University. I had received a merit scholarship that covered my tuition and books for all four years. I was off to Alabama to live out my dreams of being a veterinarian. Tuskegee was a beautiful experience for me. It was the first time I had been surrounded by so many different kinds of Black people. We were from all over the world with different skills, interests, styles, accents, and dance moves. Let me tell you, the dance moves were DIFFERENT! But we were a family, bonded by the history, strength, and perseverance of our ancestors who meticulously crafted by hand, the bricks that remained in many of the buildings where our classes were held. We were forever committed to our pledge of "Bringing Tuskegee to the World and the World to Tuskegee." Yet, I still needed to figure out exactly what that meant for me.

My time at Tuskegee proved invaluable. The friends I made, the connections I cherished, and the delicious food I ate all strengthened me in different ways. Mentally, physically, and emotionally, I found myself at Tuskegee—not the me the world wanted or even needed me to be. I found who I authentically was. At Tuskegee, I fell in love with me.
I graduated from Tuskegee in May of 2015. At my graduation, I was reminded of my purpose in the world. My amazing commencement

speaker, First Lady Michelle Obama, stood at the podium, delivering a powerful message to my class. Throughout her speech, the room filled with laughter, silence, and cheers as she reminisced with us about late-night meals, crazy homecomings, and those calls to our parents for a few more dollars to buy our ramen noodles for the month. She spoke about her challenges as the first Black First Lady, the names she was called, the stares she received, and the negative stereotypes the media used to portray her. *Black. Woman. Disadvantages.* She went on to discuss her various campaigns, how she stuck beside President Obama during the hardest times, and how she cared so graciously for her daughters. I admired her. Poised, professional, accomplished. I saw myself in her. I listened intently as she finished her closing statement, etched in my memory forever. She said, "As you go out into the world to do amazing things, don't forget to bring someone up with you. Reach back into your community and help someone else." Challenge accepted.

Thirty days later, I was off to the University of Wisconsin-Madison to continue my education in their Dairy Science program as a master's student. I was eager and a little nervous, heading to a new state, needing to make new friends, and putting myself out there in a different way. I was fully engaged in my research, learning more than my brain could handle daily in classes, and only two hours away from home, but something was missing. I had made new friends, had a new daycare job that I enjoyed, but I didn't feel fulfilled yet. "Bring Tuskegee to the World and the World to Tuskegee." "Reach back into your community." It was as if my lightbulb went off. I needed to get connected to the community. That year, I decided to run for the External Vice President of the Black Graduate and Professional Student Association, where I would oversee our work within the community. I was elected to the position and was excited to get connected. I decided that in this role, I would host a Historically Black College and University (HBCU) Fair for high school students. That year, I hosted the first HBCU Fair with over 300 students from different schools around the area. As I watched our students dance, laugh, and learn together, my spirit was filled.

I continued to do different work within the community after I graduated and took a full-time role as the Dairy Youth Specialist at the University of Wisconsin-Madison. By this time, I was on several boards in the community. I became a member of Alpha Kappa Alpha Sorority Incorporated, and I was well integrated personally and professionally. I was serving on the board of the Charles Hamilton Houston Institute, a local non-profit organization, as their grant writer when a particular grant caught my attention. It was a grant for mentoring organizations to support violence prevention in the community. "Dear Diary, it's time."

I approached the board to ask if I could write this grant for a mentoring program that I had written in college. I had written the program as a freshman at Tuskegee University because it was the program I wished I'd had before I got to college. I remember writing it and thinking, "High school and college would have been so much easier if I had someone to talk to about the different things I was dealing with. If I was around other Black girls who were also going through the same thing. I wish I had a space where I could be myself as I would in my diary, out loud." One board "yes" and one $60,000 grant approval later, Dear Diary Inc. was born.

A Year of Yes
Dear Diary Inc. was officially started in January 2019. I had a staff of two, myself included, seeking to serve fifteen Black girls annually. Our mission was to help Black girls and women write their own narrative for social and economic advancement.

"Welcome to Dear Diary: Mentoring for Black and Brown Girls." I felt a sense of joy and pride introducing the organization to our new group

of twelve at our local community center. All of the girls were from the local neighborhood and all identified as Black. Our session for the day focused on voice and choice, highlighting the importance of speaking up for yourself and others, even if it makes those around you uncomfortable. We were empowering our girls to be brave, respectful, and courageous. One of our girls stood up. "Yanna, you said Dear Diary's mission was to help Black girls write their own narrative right? If that's true, why is it Mentoring for Black AND Brown girls? Why do we (Black girls) always have to share our spaces with others? We have a very unique experience, but we never have spaces just for us. We are always in spaces for Black youth including the boys, spaces for girls of color including Brown girls, or spaces for girls grouping us with everyone else. But none of these spaces really are just for us. We always feel like outsiders in spaces that are supposed to include us." I froze. The little girl in me arose, clapping. For the first time, she felt seen. I knew exactly what this young lady meant. I had experienced it myself, but I didn't have the language nor the courage to challenge the adults around me. I watched the other girls nod and respond. Agreeing with her, even cheering her on for speaking up for them. My assistant director looked at me, nervously. A smile on both of our faces at the same time. This is exactly what we had hoped we would be! We immediately changed our tagline and, in the moment, created our first core value: Services to Black girls first. Regardless of what we did as an organization, we would ALWAYS be of service to Black girls. If we couldn't proudly proclaim that, we wouldn't move forward with any initiative, partnership, or funding opportunity. At that moment, our girls tested my leadership! They challenged me to be the leader I said I would- to be bold. With their support and trust, with immense fear, I jumped into being the SHE-EO of Dear Diary, Inc.

During this time, I was still working full-time and running Dear Diary in the evenings and on weekends. By the summer of 2019, we had secured additional funding and were growing as an organization. Proud was an understatement for how I felt. With funding challenges no longer looming, I was able to initiate some of the goals I had for the organization. I started by adding two girls from our program to our board, making them full, voting board members, and paying them for their time. The organization was for them, so why shouldn't they be empowered to make decisions on how the organization operated. We partnered with their families, offering them support and resources as well as opportunities to attend programming with us. We created programs and events that were high quality, fun, and responsive to our girls and their experiences. We wrapped our arms around our staff as well. Many identifying as Black women themselves, with traumatic workplace experiences. We invited them to bring their authentic selves into our spaces, creating autonomy while still being sure that people were held accountable. We created a six-month parental leave policy, a 45-day miscarriage leave, two two-week paid mandatory rest and recharge vacations, paid every staff member a livable salary, and aligned our work schedule with the school calendar to allow parents to be off when their kids were out of school. We advocated fiercely for our girls, standing in the gap at their schools, local governments, and even with their families. We were unstoppable. I wanted this organization to do it differently. I wanted to go above and beyond, challenge the status quo, and defy norms in business. We were well on our way.

In October, I started my annual planning for the next year. Typically, I'd start planning in October, finish by Thanksgiving, take time off for the holidays, then hit the ground running in January. This year was no different. I had just begun my planning when my mentor mentioned that she was reading "Year of Yes" by Shonda Rhimes. By now, you know how much I love to read, but what you don't know is how much I equally love Shonda Rhimes. Come on now, don't you want to be a Gladiator in a Suit? Anyway, I immediately ordered the book and decided it would be my next read. The book is about how Shonda spent an entire year saying yes to all the things that scared her. I decided that I'd like to have a Year of Yes and deemed 2020 as that year.

We all remember that 2020 was a CRAZY year in every sense of the word. But for me, 2020 was my best year yet! My husband and I moved in together (we weren't married yet, but why pay two rents when we're stuck in one house together?), I was appointed to the school board, quit my job at UW-Madison, got another job, quit that job too, became the full-time SHE-EO of Dear Diary Inc., scaled our organization to over $500,000 serving over 350 girls a year, and started my consulting company, Dear Design Collaborative, a boutique business development firm pushing the boundaries of innovation and disruption to help mission-driven companies and organizations scale and become sustainable in their market. That year, in the midst of a global pandemic, I was the healthiest I'd ever been (running and cooking good food was my pastime), I had made the most money I'd ever made, and I was the freest I'd ever felt. I've asked myself, "What was so special about that year? What changed?" What I learned in 2020 during my Year of Yes was the greatest lesson of my life. I learned to say yes to *being me*.

The View from the Top
Throughout my life, I have climbed a series of mountains. Not real mountains because, well, I'm scared of heights, but that's not the point here. I've climbed life's mountains. The peaks and valleys of success and failure are all too familiar to me. Climbing to the top of these mountains, however, isn't actually the difficult part. It's getting to the top and realizing that it isn't what you thought it would be. You are so far away from the bottom that the people you've left behind look like ants, but there's still another mountain to climb. Another business to build, more people to help, another goal to accomplish. You realize that while you know the bottom well, the top is still a mystery. Don't get me wrong; I have enjoyed my accomplishments, tackling problems and overcoming challenges, but more than anything,

I've enjoyed the journey. That was the exciting part. The people I've met. The places I've gone. The things I've done. The battles I've fought. The memories I've created. There are always more mountains, always a new top. But each climb shapes the person you become, and only you can truly understand the view from the top.

Plot Twist: My Greatest Advantage

I started this chapter sharing my dream for my future. This is the life I am manifesting for myself right now. I've spent the first 15 years of my adult life working hard to prove to myself and the world that being a Black woman is not a disadvantage, seeking to lead by example for others to do the same. My commitment to excellence, persistence, and healthy disruption have helped me to become a force for community and progression. But moreover, it has helped me to experience life, love, and my own happiness. Living out my own values, loving the life I wake up to, and living my dream life out loud has been exhilarating. I want to thank my aunt for her "warning" on that day. It wasn't a warning, but an invitation. An invitation to disrupt a narrative that was never mine. She changed my life forever. She helped me to see that my greatest advantage is being authentically Me. A. Black. Woman.

Kalyanna

Kalyanna (Yanna) Williams is an entrepreneurial powerhouse and beacon of empowerment. Holding a BS from Tuskegee University and an MS from the University of Wisconsin-Madison, Yanna seamlessly blends her unique science background with her personal values and real-world business acumen to inspire change and action.

As a visionary founder and SHE-EO, Yanna is at the forefront of social entrepreneurship, offering fresh perspectives on business development, mentorship, and community building. In 2018, she launched Dear Diary, Inc. a mentoring organization dedicated to empowering Black girls to write their own narrative for social and economic advancement. Dear Diary currently serves over 300 girls annually. Following this, in 2020, Yanna unveiled Dear Design Collaborative, a boutique consulting firm that has worked with more than 25 small businesses and nonprofits through expert business development and operations strategies leading to increased scalability and long-term sustainability. Keen on solving real problems and staying ahead of future problems, Yanna recently launched The Group Chat Social Club, a vibrant global online community for Black women aimed at fostering connections, collaboration, and community and committed to ending loneliness in successful Black women.

While Yanna loves her busy life as a businesswoman, she finds no greater joy than spending time with her husband and son nestled in a book in their Arizona home or traveling the world and creating lasting memories.

How to connect with Kalyanna:
LinkedIn: https://www.linkedin.com/in/kalyanna-williams-ab103375/

Narration on Kalyanna
with Cortney

Rewrite your stories, rewrite your life

It's early 2010 and I just left my performance review with my manager. As always, I am disappointed by my measly three percent raise, which is the company standard. Every year I go in with high hopes that this is the year I am going to be promoted and recognized for all my hard work. Luckily for me, I have a coaching call with my new mentor later that day. Of course, I am hoping she is going to side with me. I can vent about how management is dumb not to see all my good qualities and she can tell me how I deserved to be promoted.

But that's not how the conversation went down.

Instead, she says to me, "I don't want you to aspire to get a five percent raise and be promoted to the next level. I want you to set your sights so much higher. Next year, you will get a twenty percent raise and be promoted to a senior level manager."

That was laughable to me. At the time, I wasn't even a salaried employee. I was being paid by the hour and contributing at an individual level. Being promoted to a senior level manager was nowhere near achievable in my mind. It wasn't even on my radar.

Bingo – that was the problem.

The problem wasn't management.
The problem wasn't because I wasn't working hard enough (because I was).
The problem was MY STORY.
I crafted a story to tell myself that I wasn't worthy; I wasn't smart; I wasn't good enough.
I had no problem believing I was a hard worker – which only gained me hard work.
I was begging for scraps when I should have been exuding confidence.
The Universe listens to your frequency and gives you the exact match.

We are a culmination of the stories we tell ourselves.
Our external world is a direct match to our stories and beliefs.
I can look at most people's lives and pretty accurately predict the stories they consistently tell themselves.

Take a moment and listen to your story about your body:
I'm fat. I'm weak. I'm sick. I'm tired.
Is that close?

Take a moment and listen to your story about money:
Money doesn't grow on trees. Money is the root of all problems. I have to work hard for money. I only have enough to get by. I will never make enough money.

If you are not deliberate in your thinking, then you are subject to what the masses are thinking about that topic. Most times, the masses come from a place of struggle and their thinking is fear-based. Be the one that comes from a place of love, not fear.

When you rewrite your stories, you rewrite your life.

It is the fastest, most direct route to living the life of your dreams.

By the way, the year after I had that life-changing conversation with my new mentor, I was promoted to a senior level manager. That conversation changed the way I saw myself and I never looked back. Within five years of that conversation, I went from being an hourly employee to making six-figures a year. And the truth is, I stopped working hard.

BETH + PAMELA
Yin and Yang

Promise me you'll always remember:
"You are braver than you believe,
and stronger than you seem,
and smarter thank you think"

– Christopher Robin to Pooh

Beth + Pamela

Yin and Yang

Pamela

It was the summer of 1973; I was three years old. I remember my father holding my face, looking deep into my eyes and saying, "You are our chosen one." I didn't know what it meant, but from the warmth of his hands, I knew it was good. It made me feel special. That was the first time I remember hearing the word "adopted". My parents adopted me at five months old from the Washington, D.C. foster care system. They did a wonderful job early on making sure that I knew adopted meant wanted and not unwanted.

That summer, my father got a job opportunity that moved us to a new upcoming urban area called Reston. It was a planned community, envisioned to be racially integrated—a provocative idea at a time when most communities were either formally or informally segregated. My parents wanted an opportunity for our family to grow up in a diverse community.

We moved into our quaint Reston home. Shortly after, a new family moved into the yellow house next door. Once settled, it was only appropriate for us to meet our neighbors throughout the cul-de-sac. Mom and Dad made friends rather quickly. There weren't a lot of kids my age in the neighborhood, except for right next door. The girl in the yellow house was the same age as me. And she had a cat. That was the first time I pet a cat and felt the unconditional love from an animal. I knew I would always want to be around them.

Beth, the little girl in the yellow house, was my first friend. I did not know yet that she would forever be the yin to my yang, the peanut butter to my jelly, the macaroni to my cheese, my best friend for life.

Beth

Strength comes in many forms: physical, emotional, mental. For me, strength has always come from my friendship, my sisterhood, my stronger than blood BOND with my best friend, Pam. Pam and I met in January 1973, at the age of three when my family moved in next door to hers in Reston, Virginia. Our weary mothers were SO happy that their daughters had a built-in playmate so close by! We are exactly the same age... actually Pam is 17 days older than me. I don't remember the exact day that we met, but I can't remember a day after that we weren't together.

We are as different as can be: I'm white, she's black; I'm short, she's tall; I'm introverted, she's extroverted. But we share the same thoughts, the same outlook on life, the same heart. We finish each other's sentences, almost like twins. We even have mental telepathy – many times I'm thinking about calling her and I pick up my phone, and there she is calling me.

Beth and Pamela as children

Or we're sitting talking and fall silent, and a completely random thought comes into my mind like, "I wonder how Paula is doing." We hadn't been talking about Paula, mind you, but Pam picks up on my thoughts and will suddenly say, "Have you talked to Paula recently?" It's spooky!

There's a line in the movie *Rocky*, where he's asked what makes his relationship with Adrian work. He responds, "She fills gaps." "What's gaps?" he's asked. "She's got gaps, I've got gaps, together we fill gaps." That's my bestie and me, she's the yang to my yin, the Thelma to my Louise, the other half of my soul.

Growing up my mom called us "two peas in a pod". Our names, when our parents would call out to us at each other's homes, were either Pam/Beth or Beth/Pam. We both answered to either one. All through elementary, junior high, and high school, we spent just about every afternoon, night, and weekend together. We'd ask our parents, "Can Pam stay for dinner?" or "Can Beth stay over tonight?" We weren't asking for permission, rather we were letting our parents know where to find us.

Pamela

Growing up black in a predominantly white area was not easy. When my parents moved across town, it was difficult not being right next door to Beth. Whether I ate at her house or she at mine, our parents were constantly dropping us off at each other's houses!

When we began going to school, my parents enrolled me in a private school. Beth went to public school. I was one of only four black kids in the entire school; needless to say, I did not feel like I fit in. My parents wanted the best schooling for me, but at what cost? I was bullied, teased, and just felt invisible. I didn't excel academically. Reading was tough for me. Especially when I had to read out loud in front of my peers. When I got to a long word, I could hear the smirks and giggles. I hated it when the teacher called my name. I never raised my hand. My favorite subject was PE, because this was my opportunity to SHINE!

One day my PE teacher pulled me aside and asked, "Have you heard of Wilma Rudolph?" "No", I replied. "You run just like her, fast as lightning! She was the fastest woman in the world in the 1960s. Won gold medals in the Olympic Games!" "Really?" I asked. "Yes, you should look her up when you get home." And that's exactly what I did. The one thing he didn't tell me is that she was black. A black American woman who exceeded all the odds. A few days later, that same teacher asked if I was interested in running for the track team. I said, "YES!" This was the first time I didn't feel invisible and, instead, I was seen for my gift. I broke records. People cheered for me. I felt joy.

Beth

I developed early, around age 11, and switched from a skinny kid to a well-rounded fuller young woman. I was very self-conscious about my changing body and became extremely shy in junior high and high school. Pam was my protector. She wouldn't allow anyone to make fun of me. She was my interpreter. She knew how I felt, so if someone asked a question, she'd quickly speak up to answer as I was unable to speak unprovoked to anyone. Even if provoked, I'd freeze up! I remember days I'd stay home from school "sick," and my mom would tell me to call a classmate and find out the homework assignment. I literally couldn't do it! I couldn't pick up the phone and call someone. My shyness handcuffed me and defined me for SO many years!

Pamela

I'm so glad my mother listened to me one evening while we were in the kitchen: "Mom, I no longer want to be in private school. I don't feel like I belong!" We cried and she felt my pain, not really knowing it had been so bad. My father didn't want me to leave private school, but he finally agreed, and I went to public school for the first time in seventh grade. I was so excited for new friends and mostly to be going to school with Beth!

From junior high through high school, Beth and I were rarely apart. I was labeled the vocal one, "jazz hands" if you will. Beth was shy and more reserved. But because we were glued at the hip, we were a force to be reckoned with.

Although I made friends easily, I never wanted to join a group or be a part of a club. It reminded me of my peers staring and judging me in private school. I hated feeling insecure as I navigated myself through the differences between public and private school. But Beth was always there to help me through all the teenage years coming-of-age stuff: academics, boys, body changes, acne!

As a fifteen-year-old, my parents encouraged me to join a club or play a sport; I ended up getting a job a local roller-skating rink instead of joining an extracurricular activity. It was a great first job; I thought I was so cool working at the coolest teenager hang-out in town. This was my first taste of understanding the freedom of making my own money. When I got my first paycheck, I purchased my first pair of Jordache jeans! :-) Life was good. Beth started working around the same time, and we both loved the idea of having our own money. We'd dream together while walking to the local plaza for lunch or taking the bus to the mall to buy new clothes. It was the first time we really enjoyed the fruits of our labor. Beth saved and purchased a 1981 Volkswagen Rabbit, stick shift! No one could drive a stick shift, but Beth could! We were off, now able to explore and dream more.

Beth and I graduated high school, and I went off to college. I was totally devastated that Beth couldn't come with me. My parents encouraged me to go to an all-black college in southern Virginia. I agreed only because I would still be driving distance from Beth.

Beth

In the fall of 1988, Pam and I went to different colleges around six hours apart. That was my first foray into the big bad scary world without her! She went to St. Paul's College, a very small predominantly black college in southern Virginia, right next to the North Carolina border. I went to the University of Delaware, a large school of around 11,000 students, two hours north of home. When I first received my college acceptances, I learned I was also accepted into George Mason University, which was around 25 minutes from home. That's where I REALLY wanted to go! But my mom convinced me to go away, as she really wanted me to have the "full college experience." According to her, if I went to GMU, I'd be too close to home to justify paying for room and board on campus. But if I lived at home and commuted to school, that wouldn't give me the full experience *she* wanted for *me*.

Oh, how I wished I had gone to GMU! At Delaware I was nameless, faceless, and a dot in the crowd. I was housed in a quad dorm room with three other women, and it was everything that terrified me about life rolled up into one. I couldn't make any friends, probably because I confined myself to my dorm room as much as possible! I ate (I gained the "freshman 25," not just 15!), I slept, and I left town almost every weekend – either to go home or down to visit Pam for the weekend. At the end of the semester, my mom finally gave in to my pleas to come home and transfer to GMU. However, I did so poorly at Delaware that only three measly credits transferred. After that, I never went back to finishing my degree. It was my first lesson in realizing I had to fight and advocate for myself.

Pamela

Although I started college with a lot of insecurities, I ended up joining a sorority and made a lot of new friends! But nothing compared to the safe place I felt when I was with Beth. I majored in Business with a minor in Psychology. Those four years in college went by so fast. Since academics was never my thing, I was eager to graduate so I could tackle the real world with my bestie close by.

Beth

After Pam graduated college in 1992, she moved back to Reston, where I'd entered the workforce three years earlier. Finally, we were back together again full-time! Our friendship was just as strong, but the time away from each other allowed me to grow. I had learned to be more self-sufficient, more self-reliant. I started learning who I was; the Beth part of Pam/Beth.

Pamela

After college, I was so blessed that my first job was working for a woman who ran the whole corporation; she oversaw all the *men* and women in the company which was rare in those days. For four years, I was able to watch her create, make decisions, lead and not follow. I wanted to be just like her. She encouraged me to do so. Other jobs came and went throughout the years, and each of them was a building block towards fulfilling my dream.

By spring of 1998, I was growing in a challenging position that had me meeting famous, prominent people from all over the world. My parents were overjoyed! They hoped I would retire from this company. Right after receiving a big promotion, I made an announcement to my parents that evening in their kitchen that I would be quitting this job to start my own business. OMG, the look on their faces. My mother had a blank stare for what seemed like 15 minutes. And I thought I might have to resuscitate my father. Then, my mother calmly said, "What business are you looking to start sweetheart?" I boldly said, "A pet sitting business, and I hope to start it with Beth!" She said, "A pet sitting business?" I'll never forget the look of disappointment on their faces! My father chimed in, "Why would you ever want to stop working with famous people?" I explained, "I'd love to be famous myself one day! I can do this Daddy, trust me."

My parents knew I wasn't asking them if I could quit my job. I was telling them I'm going to quit my job and that was the end of the story. Actually, it was the *beginning* of the story.

After all these years of having academic troubles, insecurities, and not feeling a part of anything, life finally made sense! Those challenges created a drive in me, and I knew I wanted to be an entrepreneur! And an entrepreneur with my best friend Beth.

I couldn't wait to tell her my idea.

Beth
Pam came to me one day in April 1998 and suggested we start a pet sitting business. I had just interviewed for a job at the company where she'd been working for five years, and she thought pet sitting could be a nice side hustle. On the drive home from my interview for the "day job" we came up with our business name, Best Friends Pet Care, and our motto, "Your best friend is our best customer!"

We dove in head-first, made up brochures, got a website and email addresses, and off we went! Our first 50 clients were all from word-of-mouth. We were growing so quickly that just eight short months later we quit our jobs to focus full-time on our new business.

It was January and there was only one problem: January is the slowest time of year for pet sitting! Even so, I had no doubts we'd succeed. Why? Pam! Her optimism was contagious, and she had visions that we would become the "biggest and BEST pet sitting company in Northern Virginia!" We made mistakes in the beginning – SO MANY mistakes! We navigated our way through it and made our own rules.

One of the smartest things we did was divide up our duties based on our strengths. I was always very good with numbers and very organized, so I managed our books. Pam was a great communicator and a natural saleswoman, so she brought in the customers. We worked hard and just stared at anyone who warned us, "Don't go into business with your best friend! Either the business won't survive, or the friendship won't survive!" We'd respond, "Well that would be a shame for the business to fail, but our friendship could survive a nuclear blast!" That's how confident we've always been in the strength of our friendship!

In June 1999, we got a letter in the mail that seriously threatened to derail our business. It was from an attorney informing us that "Best Friends Pet Care" was a federally trademarked name, and we were in violation. We had 30 days to cease and desist using it! We cried, we cursed, we pulled our hair, and searched for answers. We brainstormed 30 other possible names. In the end we decided on "All Friends Pet Care," so we could still keep our motto. It also moved us up in the alphabetical listings! Bonus! AND it conveyed that we cared for all pets, not just dogs. The best was when the attorney reached back out to ask us to turn over the website domain we owned for Best Friends Pet Care. We said they could have it…for a price! We not only grew stronger from this experience, but we also made a profit!

Pamela
When I hear the phrase "Everything Happens for a Reason," I think about Siesta Key. Beth and I stumbled across this magical place on the gulf coast of Florida in May of 2000. Who knew all these years later, it's not only ranked one of the most beautiful beaches, but holds the key to our heart, soul, and mind. Whether it's managing our business, or dealing with life challenges, Beth and I use Siesta Key to focus on what we love most: our sisterhood. This is our time to reconnect and restore, laugh while the sun is rising, and lay our heads on each other's shoulder and cry while the sun sets. There is not a year that goes by when we don't visit Siesta - our sanctuary, our retreat, our safe place. I see us growing old and gray holding hands staring at the ocean talking about how GREAT GOD IS!

Beth
One of my biggest challenges to date was when I was diagnosed with a very rare and aggressive form of uterine cancer at the age of 43. I had a full hysterectomy where the surgeons removed everything. They sent

it out for testing, and it was a miracle that the cancer had not spread. I wouldn't have made it through that time without my bestie by my side. She was with me from the initial diagnosis to the oncology appointments, to the pathology results even though she was in the midst of planning her wedding and starting a brand-new life. She would remind me daily NOT to worry about my maid of honor duties. She kept me focused and positive as she lifted me up when I was consumed with the "what ifs." With her reminders, I was able to take it one day at a time.

One of the blessings that came out of this situation was I began spending time at the gym to become healthier. I began to fall in love with group fitness, particularly indoor cycling. Pam challenged me to consider becoming an instructor. When she first said to me, "You love the classes so much, why don't you become an instructor and teach them?" Teach them??? ME??? Me who can't talk to people or look them in the eye? Or...could I? Had I really grown that much?

Like many times in the past, it was *her* encouragement that led me to attend a Spinning Certification. I took a Schwinn Certification a few months later, and in June 2016, I got certified in the Les Mills cycling program, RPM. I have since added the Les Mills HIIT class, Sprint, and their mind/body class, BodyBalance, to my list of certifications. Almost ten years later, I am still a proud fitness instructor. I am still full-figured, still dealing with my own body insecurities, still struggling at times with talking in front of people, yet I teach between five to six classes per week. I LOVE it! It would have NEVER happened without encouragement from my bestie!

Pamela

After all the ups and downs, Beth and I just celebrated 26 years in business together. The story is a book of its own. We could fill countless pages of what we've gained, lost, laughed, and cried about. In those 26 years of business together, we have supported each other through relationships, marriages, sickness... Today, Beth and I are in a beautiful season of life, as our entrepreneurial spirits have led us to another business adventure together.

Beth

Earlier this year, Pam and I launched Monarchs in Motion, dedicated to helping women entrepreneurs in the pet sitting industry. Our motto is "Self-care means business!" and we are promoting the need to care for one's SELF in order to improve both your personal AND business life. We speak from a place of authenticity and raw experience.

Pamela

We chose the monarch butterfly as our symbol for its beauty, transformation, hope, and personal growth, which is what Beth and I have lived in our lifetime together.

Beth

I don't think you ever fully "figure it out." You just grow as you change, and you learn how your strengths are best adapted to your challenges. And, if you are very, very lucky, you have a best friend, a sister, a ride-or-die, to fill your gaps and fall in step with you on this journey called life.

Beth + Pamela

Beth Greenberg Cotell is a business owner, fitness instructor, and professional dog mom. She lives with her husband, David, and their four canine children. She also volunteers with HEART, a Siberian husky rescue group, as she has a particular passion for the breed. Beth graduated from the university of hard knocks. She has a major in life experience and a minor in creating the change you want to be. She lives by Yoda's words: "Do. Or do not. There is no try!"

Pamela Ahart-Steward strives to find joy in the little things and do whatever makes her soul happy. Shortly after graduating from St. Paul's College with a degree in Business and a minor in Sociology, she discovered her desire to be an entrepreneur. It was not easy as she navigated through low self-esteem and self-worth as a young adult. With God's help, she took a leap of Faith and never turned back. Her passion led her right to her purpose. Happily married to her husband Anthony, she enjoys working out, dancing, volunteering, and journaling in her free time.

In 1998, Pam and Beth co-founded All Friends Pet Care (AFPC), a professional in-home pet sitting business in Northern Virginia. Today, they proudly run AFPC side-by-side, despite everyone's warnings that "you don't want to go into business with your best friend!" In early 2024, they also co-founded Monarchs in Motion, where they support female pet-industry business owners while simultaneously emphasizing the importance of self-care. As head coaches, they help women entrepreneurs achieve success in their business while maintaining a healthy work-life balance.

How to connect with Beth + Pamela:
Instagram:
allfriendspetcare
monarchsinmotion

Facebook:
AllFriendsPetCare
MonarchsNMotion

Email:
topdogs@allfriendspetcare.com
hello@monarchsinmotion.com

Narration on Beth + Pamela
with Cortney

Discover your superpowers

When I am working on something, like this book for example, I get lost and completely absorbed in the task at hand. I've been accused a time or two of being a workaholic, spending hours on end in my office churning out content for books and classes that I am creating. I've always taken slight offense to the term workaholic – as when people say it to me, they aren't saying it in a good way.

I've come to realize that when I am creating for eight, ten, or twelve hours at a time, it's one of my unique gifts. It's a strength. I can focus for long periods of time on one thing. I am in the zone and get lost where time doesn't exist. In fact, when I look at the clock and see that it's 6pm and I am still in my pajamas from the morning when I sat at my desk twelve hours earlier, I get anxious. Not because I'm judging the moment, but because I feel the pressure of the outside world to live within the idea of working 9-5. Of course, any strength overplayed becomes a weakness. But this level of focus is one of the many superpowers I have uncovered for myself over the last few years.

In a world that often emphasizes the importance of overcoming weaknesses and striving for balance, the idea of leaning into one's strengths might seem counterintuitive. However, focusing on and developing our inherent strengths can lead to greater personal fulfillment, professional success, and overall well-being. By harnessing what we naturally excel at, we can achieve our full potential, create more value in our lives, and enjoy a more satisfying journey of personal growth.

Perhaps that is why I am so obsessed with personality profiles. I not only help people discover their strengths, but I want to learn about their strengths too. Maybe that's because one of my very own strengths, according to Strength Finder, a personality profile created by Gallup, is "maximizer." People with a maximizer strength are committed to seeing both individuals and groups excel. They don't settle for mediocrity, instead, they strive for excellence. They take the good and transform it into something great. Untapped potential excites me – I look at people and naturally see what they are capable of – and usually that is tied directly to their strengths.

That is also the reason why I became certified as a Human Design practitioner. It's another profile of sorts that allows people to unpack their unique characteristics and potentials. As a 5/1 Manifestor (for all you HD nerds out there, like me), I can't help but investigate, share with others, and then execute. It's literally in my DNA.

What's in your DNA? What makes you unique? I promise you, uncovering this will help you succeed in life. Learning about your strengths will help to promote self-awareness and self-acceptance. When individuals understand their inherent qualities, they can embrace their unique capabilities without constantly comparing themselves to others. This self-acceptance fosters confidence.

I've noticed that when helping individuals discover their strengths, they often take them for granted or view them as unremarkable. This happens because these strengths are so intrinsic to who they are that they don't even recognize them. They assume everyone perceives the world the same way they do; missing the chance to leverage their unique abilities.

No one sees the world exactly like you do. You are unique with distinctive gifts to offer. If you find it difficult to identify your strengths, ask trusted friends and family members what they appreciate most about you. In their responses, you'll find clues to your true strengths and unique gifts. And you'll be on your way to finding your superpowers!

LAURA SCHUCH
Imposter Syndrome

Laura

Imposter Syndrome

I am not a torchbearer. At least, I don't think of myself as one.

I am not an archeology professor, wearing an iconic hat, searching for the Ark of the Covenant, escaping a pit of snakes and outrunning a boulder. I am not even a member of a group of unlikely pre-teen heroes on a quest for the lost treasure of One-eyed Willy with a map and a belief in friendship so strong that they literally brought what was buried back to life. No, I am not an action star like Indiana Jones or one of the Goonies. Frankly, to say I am torchbearer feels like being an Imposter.

My experience with torchbearing is more like using a flashlight to create shadow animals on the wall during a power outage. Or holding the light pointed up at your chin when telling spooky stories at slumber parties. Or lighting the path for a group of jumpy campers during a summer-camp night hike.

It was summer 1984 at Camp Ledgewood in northeast Ohio, and I was nine years old. While flashlights were on the packing list, only three of the ten girl scouts brought them. At that time, flashlights were big, plastic, and heavy. They were also rather costly to use as they required multiple D size batteries. My light-streaming hand weight was bright orange and weighty. It was one of my prized possessions as I was afraid of thunderstorms, especially when the power went out. My mom gave it to me to keep by my bed, just in case, but more likely to keep me from waking her up when I was scared. Even at the age of 9, I had a great appreciation for my flashlight. I would hold it up to my hand to try to see what was inside. My solid flesh would glow, and I could see my arteries and veins. I would think of the blood inside those vessels and remember how our blood is red (oxygenated) when it leaves the heart and is blue on the way back. I was too young to truly comprehend the complexity of the cardiovascular system, but I wanted to see if I could tell the difference between the vessels. I remember thinking that I would probably make a good doctor since I knew so much about the human body. I was still in the age of wonder and had many ideas of what I could become and do.

As we set out for the hike, my troop leaders loosely spaced the campers with flashlights and instructed us to light the path for others, so we could see any rocks or roots that might be a tripping hazard. I took that job seriously and diligently made sure to illuminate what was immediately in front of me. Occasionally, I would also scan the surrounding trees, especially if there was a noise. But my light often created odd shadows as we passed various objects which made the forest look eerie. I gripped that flashlight the whole time even though both hands ached by the end. I was scared of the forest shadows, but I was emboldened by the thought that I was really good at lighting the path for the other girls, maybe even the best. Needless to say, we did not see any animals - I am sure our boisterous tromp around the woods scared every living creature within a mile.

As I fast forward through the subsequent years of my youth, I cannot remember any other instances of feeling like a torchbearer. I didn't consider myself a leader. I struggled with confidence, self-esteem, my self-concept - whatever label you want to put on it - for many years beginning in middle school. Maybe it was because we moved frequently during my formative years. Or maybe it was my introverted, quiet nature and owning the label "shy" that most adults seemed to want to stick on me. While I was never invited to the annual Leadership Retreat in high school, I did participate in activities. Some might have considered me a band nerd, who was fairly athletic, and I got very good grades. I worked hard, and pretty much flew under the radar until my senior year.

I ended up being popular, but not exactly for the reasons most graduates want to be known for. There wasn't a senior superlative that fit me as I graduated high school six months pregnant with my oldest son (Most Likely to be a Teen Mom?). He is one of the best things in my life (he has three siblings – together they make four of the best things in my life). Even though I felt a greater bond with Hester Prinn and her scarlet letter than I did with my peers. Shortly after I graduated, I found myself navigating a new path of accelerated adulthood. I moved to Michigan with my husband (we got married in May of my senior year). He was a sophomore in college, and I took a year off to care for the baby. My plan was to start school the following fall. We lived in campus family housing, so we were somewhat insulated by living among other families trying to balance the demands of home and school, while living with very little income. It wasn't until I ventured outside campus that I encountered judgy comments.

It started innocuously at the grocery store in the checkout line with my little one in the shopping cart. Someone would see me, just barely 18 years old with the baby and say, "Wow, you don't look old enough to have a baby." As I tended to look young for my age, I'm not so sure they meant it as a compliment. It happened often, and eventually, I began to wonder if all these older, more experienced people were right. I internalized it. My perfectionist nature and low self-concept provided the perfect soil for seeds of self-doubt and insecurity. Many new parents would probably admit that there is a point at which you feel like you have no idea what to do or how to help your baby. Hopefully you have support through family and resources. I had left my family back in Ohio and felt isolated. I started to question whether I was capable of taking care of this baby. I read everything I could – I had a handful of child rearing books and would go to the library every week (this was pre-internet) to learn more. But the negative self-talk was always there – *"Laura, you are not good enough."*

I started to anticipate implications from others that I did not meet their expectations of a mother. I avoided interacting with people in public, such as church on Sundays, because I didn't want to hear judgmental comments that would only solidify what I was already feeling about myself. I simultaneously doubled down on my desire to be a good parent. I rented VHS tapes about child-rearing. I attended seminars by psychologists. I learned about positive praise and researched the best type of toys to promote cognitive development and imaginative play. We read to our son every night. We had a nighttime routine and consistent bedtime. I did not allow my son to eat junk food (although my mom made sure he didn't miss out on ice cream). We did everything "right," but it didn't stop me from feeling like an impostor. What I did to be a good mom, didn't seem to matter to anyone else. All they saw was a young mother. And my ego listened to my shadow and convinced me they were right, *I was too young.*

This is the first time that I can pinpoint consciously trying to improve others' impressions of me. Being an impostor is more than feeling like you don't belong - that is one component. A better description for me was that I was attempting to be someone I was not. I was wearing a mask, a costume, a disguise that was a misrepresentation of who I objectively was. I feared that at some point everyone would figure out my secret. And, for me, there was a fear that they were right. I was afraid that these older, wiser adults would see me for who I really was – a scared kid that wasn't skilled or knowledgeable enough to take care of another human. I am now aware that I often "read into" what others said through my own lens of self-doubt. Any advice that was offered to me morphed in my brain to be a criticism. I became defensive, albeit internally. I started to hear through a distortion in my mind, by my ego. I stopped seeing what I was illuminating through my conscious parenting and focused on the shadows within. But this is what happens when we experience life through the imposter's mask. We block the light, even our own.

The term Imposter Syndrome was first coined by two researchers, Clance and Imes, in 1978, to describe a cognitive distortion experienced by high-achieving women. In their research, women doubted their skills, abilities and intellect. They fear being exposed as a fraud, even when there is evidence to the contrary. Researchers have since come to understand that the distortion is not limited to women, as it is most often found among members of underrepresented groups. And it is related to high-pressure situations.

The tendency to feel like an imposter stuck with me for years, decades really. When I started college, I was faced with another dilemma – am I a student like my peers, or am I a mother? As I ended up starting college at the age of 19, I looked like a typical freshman. Except my home wasn't a dorm; it had a crib, a changing table, and a highchair. The Imposter shadow lurked there too – *I was not normal.*

It seemed my interactions with people reinforced my insecurities. With each child I had, I would still hear comments like, "You look too young to have two (...three...four) children!" I *never* heard it as a compliment regardless of the other person's intent. Our perception is our reality, and my reality was built on the fear that people were going to figure out that I really didn't know what I was doing as a parent. The self-doubt might begin with concern over the proper way to feed your baby or discipline your toddler, but once your kids are school age, there are even more people – their teachers, other parents, coaches, etc. – to convince that you know what you are doing. One of the most harmful aspects of this fear is the missed opportunities for connection. I didn't simply create a wall that would allow me to hide who I really was; I created a wall that would keep everyone else far enough away.

And, when I entered the workplace, the shadow of the impostor followed. Even though I had enough education (graduate degree) to meet the requirements for a position, and ample experience, I still felt like at some point my employer and coworkers would figure it out – *I am not qualified*. In some positions I held, I often thought there was someone else there that would be better than me. The Imposter showed up in so many areas of my life. And it was lonely.

Fortunately for me, I experienced a divine disruption. The Universe stepped in to remind me of who and what I really am. Like when my mother gave me a flashlight to help me manage my fears as a child, I was given something that would eventually bring light to the shadows and shatter the mask of the Imposter. But it wouldn't be a quick fix, and it would require commitment.

I was in my first role as a manager. I am not sure if it was the exhaustion of wearing the mask while I managed staff, but the Universe decided to give me a strong nudge - I experienced a dark night of the soul sparked by the unexpected loss of my mother. She was my best, and longest, friend; the person who knew immediately if there was something wrong by the way I said, "Hello?" when answering the phone. She saw through the mask. The loss was deep and dark. The mask became so heavy and confining.

I questioned my relevancy and existence. What am I doing? What is my purpose? Am I living the life that I want to live? These and other similar questions became my focus. I read Eckhart Tolle's *The Power of Now* and Michael Singer's *Untethered Soul*. And I started meditating in the traditional Zen tradition.

Meditation became my flashlight, and the path within me became illuminated. Through meditation, I was guided into remembering who *I Am*. It wasn't a strong beam at first, more like a flicker. Curiosity was my traveling companion. I dipped my toes into any topic that peeked even a little interest. I gained a whole new vocabulary. I tested the waters of interacting with like-minded souls.

And, with each new topic I explored, I learned more about myself. Some things resonated, but others didn't. The simplicity of Zen spiritualism, with a focus on Being, presence, and mindfulness clicked, and my beam got a little stronger. I noticed that it was easier to drop into a meditative state. I also didn't seem to worry as much – about most things – but especially what other people thought. I had profound moments of clarity and a sense of connectedness to things greater than me. I loved playing with focusing on presence and meditation and how it impacted my interactions at work. I loved the woozy detached feeling of mindful nothingness. Yet, I didn't talk about my new interests much. I kept the mask, which transfigured to a shape to keep my new passions a secret. *The Imposter still needed a disguise.* I loved who I was becoming, but what if others didn't?

Eliminating the Shadows

Meditation connected me with my true nature. That alone is a major hurdle in the path to living authentically, but it isn't the only requirement. If one is to truly carry a light for others, they must live with authenticity. Authenticity is the perfect combo of knowing who you are and living that truth in all aspects of your life. It means allowing the internal to be seen. It means sharing your thoughts and experiences. It means openness and being present. Authenticity happens through sending beams of light to the shadows within and working through what lurks there. It can be unsettling to approach what is in the dark, but the Universe provides a map to guide anyone who seeks. What that map looks like will vary for each person. For me, that map included an adventure that I never imagined.

Before continuing with my story, I am going to ask that we take a brief pause together...

Sit back in your chair...

Take a deep breath...

Now hold your left hand out – palm towards you. Find the spot on the side of your wrist, directly below your pinky finger. Take your right thumb and gently press that hollow space. If you are having a hard time finding the spot, bend your hand back and forth. The spot is in the crease of the wrist. Gently hold your thumb there for 3 to 5 breath cycles. Relax and breathe.

You are pressing the acupressure point called Heart 7 (HT7). It is the seventh point on the Heart meridian. This point is a powerful point for anxiety, stress and insomnia. It is also called Spirit Gate and is a Window to the Sky point, as it connects us to our higher self. This point is key for those experiencing heart problems, which isn't surprising as it is on the heart meridian. In Traditional Chinese Medicine (TCM), there are twelve meridians, each is associated with an organ. The organs function in pairs, which relate to one of the five elements – fire, water, earth, metal, and wood. Fire is the exception. It is the only element related to *four* meridians. In addition to the heart, fire is associated with the small intestine, the pericardium (or heart protector) and the triple heater.

From a spiritual perspective in TCM, fire is our *shen*, or spirit. According to Dr. Aminah Raheem, founder of Soul Lightening Acupressure (now Insight Acupressure), an acupressure program based on the five elements, fire manifests as the individual and unique expression of the divine flame. It relates to inspiration and intuition and helps us move beyond the promptings of the ego.

As stated by Dr. Raheem :
"In our hearts we carry our own individual spirits. Inspiration and intuition, associated with the heart and fire, help us to remember that spirit. And this spirit comes forth from each of us in a unique way. To come into individuation, one much follow one's own heart, one's own fire, and one's own spirit – in short, to follow what brings joy to one's heart is to follow the self."

If you haven't already, you can let go of the HT7 point. I shared this point with you for two reasons. First, to get a little taste of acupressure, a healing modality that is an excellent treatment that can easily be adapted to self-care. But there is another, more poignant reason for sharing this, acupressure was part of my map to authenticity. In addition to meditation, as previously shared, and Reiki, it has been instrumental in enhancing the light within. It has helped me dispel the shadows.

As I continued my spiritual adventure, I sought out training in Reiki. I became attuned to Reiki, and eventually became a Reiki Master Practitioner. The master level course involved sharing a complementary practice or modality that might be incorporated into our Reiki practice. One of the other students shared about acupressure, and somewhere inside me a little light turned on. That light would stay dimly lit for three years, until I took my first course in Clinical Acupressure. I was inspired by this ancient modality of healing that treats at every level – physical, emotional, mental, ancestral, etc. The program I went through, Insight Acupressure, also has a strong emphasis on the importance of empowering others by sharing protocols that are incredibly effective, yet easy and accessible. The Seva Stress Release protocol was developed for first responders and has been taught to thousands of health care professionals, but anyone can do it.

It was through self-practice of these protocols that I have experienced the most growth. I tried out protocols for deep relaxation and hormone balancing. I played with holding points when I felt stressed or in need of a restart. And the light within started to burn a little brighter. Now, the idea of sharing this knowledge through treatments or education lights me up. I have continued to complete two more courses and am currently working towards a Clinical Acupressure certification. And while I still occasionally notice Imposter-like thoughts, the transformation of my internal world has allowed me to embrace who I am and made me eager to explore more. I am able to let go of negative thoughts that used to ruminate and stick around. I have developed boundaries and I have learned to not let other people affect my energy – whether through words spoken or unspoken. I am working on expressing my thoughts and feelings in the moment and allow others to have their own impression of me. I have appreciation for who I am and who I am becoming. I am now able to write about and discuss with others my experiences with Imposter Syndrome. I am increasing my comfort level with vulnerability and have welcomed it as a companion on this great big life adventure.

In considering how to reduce or eliminate the effect of Imposter Syndrome, one could search online for tips and suggestions by those with much greater knowledge of mental health than me. I tried many of those, but they were never able to truly break through the mask. What my experience has shown me, and what simply makes sense, is to connect with your authenticity. I try not to use the term "Authentic Self." For me that is just another thing my ego likes to fixate on. If I start to ponder what my authentic self is, I easily spiral into questioning everything. Instead, I take time to connect with who I am and what brings me joy. The more I am able to be myself in each moment, the less I feel like an Imposter. It is the combination of experiencing the fullness of the present moment and finding what lights me up that leads me to authenticity. For me, that is taking a long walk in nature and reading a book. For others, it might be practicing yoga or talking with friends. The only way I would know what lit me up was to try new experiences. I was open to making mistakes; I embraced the beginner's mind. I realized it was okay to not know, to not be good at something, and to not like something that others seemed to like. I had to find my own path.

I learned to...
Turn the light on – I am exactly where I am supposed to be.
Take the mask off – I am exactly who I am supposed to be; and I always have the ability to change.
Explore the path before me, wherever that takes me. And I get to choose who will travel with me.
But most of all, I learned to Be Me. My hope is that maybe this will give you permission to Be YOU!

Laura

Laura Schuch, PhD, is a Health Geographer who loves learning about eastern practices that promote health and well-being. She is learning to allow herself to follow what intrigues her, without having an expectation for any particular outcome. That path has led to many new interests such as T'ai Chi Ch'uan and Qi Gong.

Laura is the owner of *Libella Reiki and Meditation, LLC*, a wellness practice that helps clients find balance and alignment. She is a Reiki Master, a meditation guide, and a practitioner of Clinical Acupressure (through Insight Acupressure) and Zero Balancing. As further evidence of her lifelong learner activities, Laura will be expanding her practice as a Licensed Massage Therapist when she completes her training in Fall 2025.

When not connecting with clients, Laura loves to explore local, state, and national parks and finds joy in the natural world. Earlier this year, the Universe also blessed her family with a furry friend, Tucker, a seven-year-old Wonderpup!

How to connect with Laura:
Email: laura@libellareiki.com
Website: www.libellareiki.com

Narration on Laura
with Cortney

You are not an imposter

In Reiki Level Two training, as the teacher of the class, I begin by going around the room and inviting students to share their thoughts and experiences with reiki since their level one training (which is typically one-month prior). Without fail, the discussion quickly turns into a conversation that amounts to the students feeling unsure of themselves – like an imposter. If you aren't familiar with reiki, the word reiki is two Japanese words: rei and ki. Rei means higher consciousness and ki means life force energy. Reiki is loosely translated to mean life force energy guided by Source. Based on this definition and the teachings of reiki, the individual preforming reiki isn't "doing anything" – they are simply the channel through which reiki flows. Therefore, their capabilities should not come into question, because, as I said – they aren't doing anything (reiki is).

Yet, almost every level two reiki student of mine begins the class feeling inadequate.

Why is this? It has me interested in learning more about this phenomenon known as imposter syndrome.

Imposter syndrome is a psychological phenomenon in which individuals doubt their accomplishments and have a persistent fear of being exposed as a "fraud." Despite evidence of their competence, those experiencing imposter syndrome feel unworthy of their success.

The term "imposter syndrome" was coined in 1978 by psychologists Pauline Clance and Suzanne Imes. Initially identified among high-achieving women, imposter syndrome is now understood to affect people of all genders and backgrounds. Various factors contribute to the development of imposter syndrome, including personality traits, family dynamics, and societal pressures.

Personality Traits: Individuals with certain personality traits, such as perfectionism, may be more prone to imposter syndrome. Perfectionists set unrealistically high standards for themselves and feel inadequate when they inevitably fall short. This can lead to a constant fear of failure and a belief that their success is undeserved.

Family Dynamics: Family expectations and early experiences can play a significant role in shaping one's self-perception. For instance, individuals who grew up in families that placed a strong emphasis on achievement may feel immense pressure to succeed. If they internalize the belief that they are only valuable when they excel, they may struggle to accept their accomplishments as genuine.

Societal Pressures: Societal norms and stereotypes can also contribute to imposter syndrome. For example, minority groups or individuals in fields where they are underrepresented may feel additional pressure to prove themselves, leading to feelings of inadequacy and self-doubt.

Imposter syndrome can have far-reaching effects on an individual's personal and professional life. The constant fear of being exposed as a fraud can lead to chronic stress, anxiety, and even depression. This emotional burden can hinder one's ability to perform effectively and pursue opportunities for growth.

Professional Impact: In the workplace, imposter syndrome can result in a reluctance to take on new challenges or leadership roles. Individuals may avoid seeking promotions or additional responsibilities out of fear that they are not qualified. This can stall career advancement and limit professional development. Additionally, the anxiety associated with imposter syndrome can lead to burnout, as individuals may overwork themselves to prove their worth.

Personal Impact: On a personal level, imposter syndrome can erode self-esteem and damage relationships. Constant self-doubt can make it difficult to accept praise or feel satisfied with one's achievements. This can create a cycle of negative self-talk and reinforce feelings of inadequacy. In relationships, individuals with imposter syndrome may struggle to communicate their needs or set boundaries, leading to imbalanced dynamics and increased stress.

What I've noticed when working with students and clients is that often imposter syndrome comes from this need to perform. What happens when you switch from a mindset of performing to serving? What if you are only there to be of service and bring love to the moment? This is the quickest way to melt away any thoughts about being an imposter, because we are all inherently made to love one another.

ERICA CRYSTOL
Bouncing Back from Grief and Loss

Erica

Bouncing Back from Grief and Loss

It was 2022, and the start of a brand-new year. It truly felt like a clean slate. I was finally starting to feel at peace again. Little did I know that I was about to go through one of the most difficult times of my life.

The year started off with a dream. More like a premonition. I woke up in the middle of the night during a panic attack. I was experiencing all the symptoms: gasping for air, crying, feelings of worry and uncontrollable terror. My dream felt so incredibly real! Amid the horror of it, I instantly knew that my life was going to be uprooted again.

After moving my business multiple times starting in 2019, moving my house, and making it through Covid, we were finally settling in. All moves were upgrades which is an obvious blessing, but it didn't feel like anything even close to that at the time.

I craved stability. I wanted to plant my roots and stand strong like a tree. I would later come to find out that I am a bird. I am meant to use my wings and fly; to foresee bad situations and fly far away from the storms that were to come.

After searching for my purpose for years, I was still establishing myself through my business. I didn't even know how to describe what I was doing quite yet. I was still discovering who I was and now my possessions were being boxed up again along with what also felt like my identity.

The dream, or perhaps nightmare, that I woke up from was so realistic. There was water running down all the walls in our house, from the ceiling to the floor. Our house was flooded. It looked like the inside of the Titanic as it was sinking. As crazy as it sounds, I knew it was a warning. I knew something bad was about to happen to our home and that we immediately needed to sell. We had just settled in, after moving two previous times, and I was just starting to feel rooted here. It was the perfect home, at least I had thought. But now, I had this undeniable belief, *"We HAVE to leave again."* Not long after I had experienced this vivid dream, we had an extremely heavy rainstorm. During this flash flood warning, multiple windows in our house began to leak and drip water.

This situation was making me realize that after all the loss in my life, I had not allowed myself to grieve situations from my past. The stages of grief that I had shoved down are the psychological tools used to help cope after a loss. I did not allow time to express my feelings. I did not handle things one at a time and they began to pile up. With this loss, I was feeling a culmination of all the losses that I had not processed in the past.

The stages of grief are shock and denial; pain and guilt; anger and bargaining; depression; hope and acceptance. I was now forced to move through these stages with the loss of my physical possessions. It was at this moment that I realized I had never fully moved through these stages after the loss of my father at such a young age.

Everything started after I returned home from my trip to study plant medicine in March 2022. I was told that I had less than one month to close my business's physical location. This was not my choice, as the building owner wanted to reclaim the space for expansion. After we had just decided we would put our house up for sale, my mind had to prepare for yet another change.

Although my entire world felt unstable, I managed to make some of the best business decisions of my career at this time. I did not realize how important the teachings of Haru Kuntanawa, leader of the amazonian tribe in Acre, Brazil, would be in 'real' life. I studied in person with Chief Haru to learn how to administer Hape to my clients. What I learned was now gently pushing *me* forward and it gave me hope. I began to incorporate it into my morning meditations. It allowed me to start off the day feeling calm and in control of my thoughts and actions.

Growing up, nothing was handed to me. I've always worked hard for the things that I have. I got my first job as soon as I was legally able. The idea of me purchasing my own home was unfathomable because of the stories and beliefs I had as a child and young adult. It became apparent to me that, although I did eventually purchase my own home, these beliefs that I had about my worthiness were showing up as I was being pushed from home to home and business to business. The uprooting was painful, yet necessary for me to heal.

These changes brought with them a priceless gift. It allowed me to examine my relationships with not only possessions, but also worthiness. I inspected the notion that my possessions do not define who I am. Objects are just things. My intentions, my heart, the way that I treat people, and how I would rebound from the contrast are more important than the material items (or loss of them). My heart song became, "I want to create memories with people and impact them in a way to uplift them."

The funny thing is, because I had already been through so much in my life, I had naively thought that the 'life lessons' would be over. That I was done being shaped into a soul that could help others out of my own experiences with struggle. I was so incredibly wrong. We can't control life. It's messy and unpredictable. It is full of loss and change. We can't prevent bad things from happening. We have to be ready and use our life lessons as an anchor for the storms that come to flood our homes. Our foundation is what's important. Our spirituality, friends, and family.

I understood that what was happening in the outside world was a metaphor for spiritual growth. My whole world was flooding, and I felt like I was drowning. I kept asking myself, "Why would I purposely choose to uproot my life again?" I had everything that I could want. A beautiful apothecary cabinet in the dining room, hand crafted kitchen nook, and a one-of-a-kind swing for the porch. I was angry that we had invested so much time and love in this new home. I could not deny the premonition, so we started the process, once again, of packing up our things that weren't still buried away in boxes from the previous moves.

I felt guilty for being upset. I have experienced multiple living conditions with my travels to Belize, Costa Rica, and Guatemala. I've seen poverty that most Americans could not fathom. My guilt stemmed from the fact that I was fortunate to even have a roof over my head. I have been given opportunities that most people in my travels would never have and I am so grateful for that.

We later found out, upon inspection, that the house had multiple issues including airborne black mold and asbestos. It was so bad that you could smell it in the air when it rained. This would account for the health issues that I had been experiencing. When I had the premonition dream, it was still winter and I insisted the windows stay open. I felt like I was being smothered. Maybe even suffocated. It was an eerie recollection of how my father had passed so suddenly years ago. This rightfully brought forth a wave of PTSD along with Panic Attack symptoms.

My dream, the foreshadowing, was a conduit for my guides to give me a glimpse of what was to come in the near future. This is when I learned to trust my instincts and follow my intuition. I instantly knew that it was time to spread my wings and fly away.

Even though I was in a time of contrast, I could see my growth. Depression used to suck me in like a riptide. During my travels to Belize, I found cacao. Consuming raw chocolate, known as cacao, naturally releases a hormone in our brain to help regulate mood. Developing a relationship with cacao has taught me the importance of self-care. I know I cannot pour from an empty cup. I cannot assist others if I have no energy left to give. I've realized over the years that taking care of myself is for everyone else's sake. It is an act of selflessness.

I attribute much of my growth to my travels and the people I met and practices I learned along the way. In March of 2024, I traveled to Guatemala in hopes of gaining a greater understanding of the culture. I also wanted to develop a stronger relationship with the plant medicine, cacao, since it has made such a difference in my life. Being in Guatemala was an incredibly liberating experience for me. Traveling to a foreign country where I did not understand the language was a challenge, especially since I was traveling alone. This trip was completely out of my comfort zone.

Upon landing in Guatemala, I had the instant realization that my entire life had led me to this point. I felt free. Like I could accomplish anything and live out my wildest dreams.

While I was there, I was able to tour two cacao farms. Cacao is the purest form of chocolate. It's the stage before any ingredients, like sugar, are added, which dilutes its potency. Cacao is a powerful superfood plant medicine that has been used in multiple cultures across the world. It was discovered in 1500 BC and has been a staple in the Mayan and Aztec cultures ever since. It is used for spiritual and medicinal purposes and can awaken inner guidance. Cacao is considered a psychoactive plant, which means it releases a series of positive chemicals in the brain. The release of these chemicals creates feelings of happiness and well-being. It also opens your heart chakra which is a gateway to hear your inner spirit and all its wisdom. The heart chakra is where we hold love for ourselves and for others. We cannot thrive fully if our heart chakra is blocked. Using Ceremonial grade medicines during meditations will give you a higher sense of self and increase your relationship with the other dimensions. I began to experiment with this amazing superfood in 2014 and, in 2019, I began offering it to my clients. Now, in 2024, I was meeting it in-person in the land where it grows, surrounded by the people that truly bring it to life. Since cacao is a "heart opener," it can gently encourage you to explore yourself and the people in your life. It allows you to view things from a different perspective.

I experienced four different ceremonies in Guatemala. Upon my arrival to Lake Atitlan, an elder, Tata Thomas, conducted our first fire ceremony near the water. It was an incredible welcoming and I felt very honored as he made a purposeful effort to say each one of our names multiple times.

The second circle was performed by a husband and wife, Tata Jerico and Nana Jessica, of Ka'kaw Chinimital underneath a breathtaking flower-covered trellis at our lakefront hotel. As we drank our cacao husk tea, we watched tiny hummingbirds feeding off the beautiful, fragrant flowers. Feeling the warmth beam down through the vines covering the delicate structure is something that I will never forget.

Next, we visited Ruk'u'w Ulew, a multi-generation women's collective. On our last day, we met with Utz K'aslemal, a midwives collective, ran by Nan Ixquik. Here, we were each given tobacco to smoke during the ceremony. After we finished smoking, we placed the tobacco in the circle where it was then taken and read by Nan. She validated my hardships and the insecurities that I battle. Without knowing me or my story, she explained that I am called to be a leader in my community and to share the sacred modalities including plants. While we were there, the women were able to receive a true womb blessing. The language barriers did not matter as I felt their blessing through touch and realized that words are not necessary when you are truly connected to spirit.

During my visit to Guatemala, I also spent time learning multiple hands-on techniques. We roasted the cacao beans over an open fire. We peeled the shell (husk) off each and every one and skillfully ground them into a powder. Being able to experience the process gives me greater respect for the Cacao Ceremonies that I lead in the States.

We were blessed by each one of these groups. Each person that we met was so genuine and accepting. We asked them what their thoughts were on the Western "Cacao Ceremony" movement. They are very excited about the movement. They are happy that we are sharing their sacred culture and that their families' names will live on in the process. Their graciousness only increased my respect for those honoring the Mayan (or any indigenous) people by ensuring that they are rightfully compensated for their knowledge and efforts. In my work, I prefer to learn directly from the source.

In addition to the Cacao immersions, while I was in Guatemala, I was able to take multiple tours in San Juan La Laguna. One of the tours took me to a medicinal plant garden tended by the local women. They transformed the herbs into multiple products, including skin care and edibles. This was quite familiar to me since it is how I started my business back in 2015. We toured a Mayan weaving cooperative called Casa Flor Ixcaco. We experienced a workshop where we observed the process of creating and dying the garments. The dyes were all natural and derived from local plants, herbs, fruits, and vegetables. My favorite tour was of the stingless bee sanctuary where multiple high-quality honey products are made. This included the sacred eye drops, Melipona, which I had been self-administering for years and now offer to clients.

The most profound part of the trip was my experience with the women's collective. They are a one hundred percent Mayan-owned, all female business. As soon as we approached the property, I felt overwhelmed with a feeling of security and unconditional love. I became very emotional and couldn't stop crying. I felt such a connection to these women; watching them work together in loving unison to prepare for our fire ceremony was something that sparked feelings deep inside of me. Having come from three generations of spiritually strong women, this was particularly touching to me. I imagined what it would be like to live like this. To be in business with family. All called to the same significance.

These groups spoke to God on our behalf, used their sacred modalities and medicines to bless us, laid hands on us, and shared their traditions in such a special way. I questioned my purpose many times before, but this experience helped me fully understand it. I knew why I was there. I had gained many indigenous allies and now I can proudly support these communities.

Slowly, over the course of five years, my boxes are being emptied and my possessions are finding a place again. I know now that my home is inside of me, my soul. It is not where I lay my head at night and store my belongings. It's the place that I can travel deep inside of myself to find peace when things are in turmoil. I've acquired strength over the years dealing with the stages of grief and loss. In Guatemala, I fully realized that home is the confidence within myself where I know that I am a vessel serving a purpose and that I deserve to be here on this Earth, regardless of status.

These days, I give myself grace as I realize that it is hard to see the entire picture while you're right in the middle of living it. I told myself years ago that the things that I was going through would encourage others one day. I hope to instill in others the feeling of hope. We can all transform our pain into purpose.

In September of 2025, one year away as I write this chapter, I will be celebrating ten years of my business, CrystolClear Naturals! It has been an amazingly fulfilling journey so far! I look back at my experience as I created my own bath and body-focused retail product line in 2015, added spiritual services in 2017, became a licensed Esthetician and opened my first retail shop in 2019, and then opened my first licensed spa location in 2021. I am eager for what is next! Everything is now coming full circle. As one door closes, another opens.

Like when I visited the women's collective in Guatemala, I feel fully energized to bring that community activism forward by continuing to host vendor shows to support the local small businesses in my area. I believe that providing opportunities for like-minded individuals to monetize creates empowerment.

The recent contrast in my life has only confirmed my life's purpose to serve others in achieving their wellbeing – body, mind, soul, and spirit.

Erica

Erica Crystol lives in Pittsburgh, Pennsylvania and is the owner of CrystolClear Naturals, LLC. An award-winning Wellness Spa and Apothecary Retail offering traveling services, retail, and events. The goal of CrystolClear Naturals is to create a unique experience where healing occurs both inside and out.

After decades of suffering from chronic pain with no answers in sight, Erica had no choice but to forge her own path. In doing so, she went on the most miraculous journey of her life. It took her to Belize, Costa Rica, and then to California where she studied with Chief Haru of the Kuntanawa tribe. Erica found solace in the native cultures where herbs take the place of western medicine. Now in 2024, she has been called to Guatemala for the most profound trip of her life.

Erica is on a mission to serve others who are on a similar fact-finding quest. Since 2012, Erica has worked with a diverse group of holistic entrepreneurs and alternative medical specialists from around the world. Today, as a teacher, public speaker, and co-author, she is multi-licensed and enriched with a wealth of knowledge. Erica stands strong physically, mentally, and emotionally, ready to share and empower others.

How to connect with Erica:
Facebook: crystolclearnaturals
Email: crystolclearnaturals@gmail.com
Website: https://crystolclearnaturals.com

Narration on Erica
with Cortney

Contrast has the greatest power to transform you

There is a misunderstanding in spiritual circles that you can eliminate contrast (i.e. unwanted trauma) from your life by raising your frequency. It's not true. I know it's not true because I spent the first ten years on my spiritual path thinking that once I become enlightened "enough" I will only attract love, peace, and joy. Then, I was hit by a big trauma. I couldn't understand why I attracted this. What was I doing wrong? Then I realized, I am not doing anything wrong. Contrast is part of life, regardless of how "enlightened" you are.

Contrast is the number one most beneficial aspect of human life when it comes to our growth and expansion. The advanced teaching isn't to become enlightened to avoid contrast, but to become enlightened so you can move through contrast gracefully, with ease, and quicker. Ever notice how some people hang on to contrast for a decade – still complaining about something that happened to them when they were younger?

The question is not if, but when will I fall. Because we all fall. The more I grow, the more I realize that trying to avoid this is not only impossible, but not the desire of our higher self. We are human on this physical plane to experience the full range of emotions.

I'm no longer going to resist the experiences and circumstances in my life that have the most capacity to transform me. I used to give up and give in at the first sign of struggle. I know I didn't come here to struggle, but I now ask myself, "Why is this happening? What parts of it can I alchemize."

I share this quote by Rene Daumal with my Vibration Mastery Program students at the end of our six-month journey together:

"You cannot stay on the summit forever; you have to come down again. So why bother in the first place?
Just this: What is above knows what is below; but what is below does not know what is above.
One climbs, one sees. One descends, one sees no longer, but one has seen.
There is an art of conducting oneself in the lower regions by the memory of what one saw higher up.
When one can no longer see, one can at least still know."

But one has seen. You have seen.
How will you conduct yourself the next time you fall?
Will you remember the view from the summit?

Follow the breadcrumbs

Add up everything you've learned from this book – each nugget from each Torchbearer.

Emily: You must be relentless and resilient to manifest your dreams.
Mary: Not everything is as it seems.
Ted: Use your imagination and start your day with intention.
Danielle: Do you like your life? If not, you have the power to change it.
Wesley: Seize the day; this moment is the moment.
Maryanne: Age is just a number.
Kalyanna: Write your story, not someone else's.
Beth + Pamela: Find your strengths and use them.
Laura: Don't ever let imposter syndrome stop you from being you.
Erica: You *will* fall; how quickly will you get up?

Wrap it up in a tight little ball and place it in your metaphorical pocket.

Let this be the inspiration for you to live *your* authentic life.

If you remember nothing else, remember that a Torchbearer creates his/her own path!

Forget about everything you thought you knew and start anew.
Follow. The. Breadcrumbs.

Cortney

Cortney Martinelli is a corporate trainer, speaker, educator, Reiki Master, Certified Yoga Teacher (CYT), founder of Akasha Yoga™ and author of the best-selling books: *Love, Reiki, Vibration* and *Cracked Open*. She has been supporting the wellness community for over a decade. During this time, she has worked with thousands of clients and students hosting 150+ events each year. Cortney's ultimate desire is to serve and support students, clients, teachers, employees, coaches, and athletes based on their individual goals for the future.

In addition to Cortney's vast experience within the world of wellness, she spent two decades working in the corporate arena for a Fortune 100 company. During that time, she specialized in employee engagement, communications, and education where she developed and delivered training and education to thousands of employees.

Cortney is the owner of SHINE and the Light House, an Education + Wellness Center in Kent, Ohio. Here, she spends most of her time offering wellness certifications, private sessions, and support to her community.

How to connect with Cortney
Website: www.SHINEohio.com
Email: cortney@shineohio.com
Instagram: cortney.shine

Shine

SHINE was created out of the concept to collaborate with other souls; bring their passion to life and encourage and EMPOWER them to share it with the world - SHINE!

Each year, SHINE helps many new authors articulate and share their stories with the world. If you would like to be part of a future book collaboration, visit: **www.shineohio.com/shine-books**

In addition to helping people *shine* through stories, SHINE's Education + Wellness Center (aka the **Light House**) was born in January 2020 as a way in which to share love and light with the world. Currently the center hosts 150+ events each year including classes, workshops, certifications, yoga, retreats, corporate training, private sessions, and more.

Learn more at www.shineohio.com

SHINE**BOOKS**

this book was guided by *love*

Made in the USA
Middletown, DE
04 September 2024